W.... ... Wait...

My Journey of Singleness and
Lessons for Those Waiting on
God's Promises

Nia Irvin-Smith

Sharon,
Be Encouraged!
Isa. 40:31
Nia

ISBN (paperback): 978-1507864043
ISBN (digital): 978-1483550091

Dedication

I would like to dedicate this book to my parents.

Dad – You are the epitome of hard work and determination. Your example inspires me to remain strong and pursue my dreams.

Mom – I don't know where I would be without your constant support and encouragement. Thank you for being a great example of a Godly woman in my life.

I love you both more than you will ever know.

Table of Contents

Dedication

Table of Contents

Introduction

Introduction

My heart for this book started out as a means to encourage those who are single and waiting for God to send them their spouse. In the midst of writing, my focus broadened as I realized that it isn't just singles who find themselves waiting on God to do something for them. We all end up in a waiting position at some point in our lives and it applies to a variety of situations. The waiting season can be an extremely difficult one, but it is my desire to see all people enjoy the fruit of a healthy, loving relationship with Jesus first and foremost before bombarding Him with a list of wants and desires. I truly believe God has placed this mantle on me because He wants us to better understand just how much He loves us and has great purpose for our lives, no matter what we think we are waiting on Him to do.

As you read this book, I want to be absolutely clear that there is no one prescription on how to live this life. We are all on a journey that is uniquely designed just for us. The moment we begin to look at others' journeys without seeking God's will for OUR life, we lose the essence of the very reason God created us. As we begin to compare and contrast with others, we leave a door open for toxic emotions to invade our hearts and cause us to be cold and distant towards God. Imagine how much more peace you can have when you aren't concerned about what everyone else is doing in relation to yourself. Imagine if we just focused more on ourselves and what God has for us and not what He has for other people. We will delve deeper into this subject later on but I challenge you before you read on to make a conscious decision to stop comparing yourself to others and watch how it changes your life.

Be careful to glean the Godly wisdom laid out before you without thinking that you must do something the exact way that someone else has done it. Be led by the Holy Spirit, as well as God's Holy Word which encapsulates the principles and precepts that we are to live by. The chapters that are to come are based on God's Word, divine revelations given to me by the Holy Spirit and my personal experiences. This book is to help a purpose filled, powerful group of individuals find their purpose in the Lord and walk confidently in it regardless of whether there's a ring on their left hand or not. It is to answer some of the many questions in whose answers may hold the breakthrough we need to successfully navigate the journey we must go through in order to receive our promises from God. It is to encourage, empower and minister to the hearts of those that need to know or be reassured of God's love for them. And most of all, it's to have some real talk about the struggles we face in waiting, especially in relation to singleness.

Journey with me as I tell some of my personal stories and share the life-changing lessons I've learned in this process. Let's get to the meat of what it really means to be waiting on God and how to live a fulfilling life in the meantime. There are some practical measures I will lay out in this book on how to find your place of peace until God allows this season to come to a close in your life. I am fully convinced that a change in perspective has the ability to change the course of your life and enable God to move forward in fulfilling the promises He's made to you. It is my hope that this book will aid you in that paradigm shift.

At this point, if anyone reading this book is not saved, I would like to invite you into relationship with our Lord and Savior Jesus Christ. I and many others have a personal testimony of how accepting Jesus into our hearts has changed our lives and I want you to experience it as well. His love for you goes beyond anything you could ever imagine and I know personally just how amazing it is to be in relationship with the true and living God. If you've been searching in all the wrong places to fill that empty space in your heart, or if you already believe and may just need to renew your commitment, a simple prayer of salvation will close out this introduction. I invite you to accept Jesus as your Lord and Savior today by reading and praying this prayer out loud.

Father, in the name of Jesus, I confess with my mouth and believe in my heart that Jesus is the Son of God and that He died for my sins and rose on the third day. I ask you to forgive me and cleanse me from all unrighteousness with the blood of Jesus. Thank you Father for sending Jesus to provide me with salvation, which allows me to be a new creature in Christ. I confess and believe that you heard my prayer and now I am a new creature in you. Amen.

1

Purely Single

*Therefore shall a man leave his father and his mother,
and shall cleave unto his wife: and they shall be one
flesh*
Genesis 2:24 (KJV)

I had to start this book by laying a foundation for singleness because much of the subject matter and examples that are to come have a special emphasis on single people. Waiting on God as it relates to marriage is a place of angst for a lot of people so I wanted to make sure to address that area of concern throughout this book. My journey of singleness was the catalyst to my lessons learned about waiting on God so I am passionate about bringing clarity to this area for my readers and establishing a firm foundation of God's Truth. It is here that I will tell you the beginning to my journey of singleness and we will learn about how singleness relates to understanding the season of waiting as a whole.

Due to the lack of understanding of God's Word amongst a lot of believers and the immoral society we live in, we can easily be oblivious to the truth of a matter according to God. So for starters, the foundational definition of a single person is one who is unmarried. Under this definition it's easy to see how single spans a large group of people who may actually be in different unmarried relationship statuses. Unfortunately, there is a growing abundance of people who are not married but don't consider themselves single. Now we know people have opinions and may feel entitled to them, but the truth of the matter is that marriage is the only relationship in which God recognizes the two people as one entity. If you are not one with another person of the opposite sex in God's eyes, then you are *single*.

Now this may not be an easy truth to accept, especially for those that may be in what they consider a loving relationship with a boyfriend or girlfriend. In this relationship they may call each other husband and wife, live together, and/or have children together and much of this is accepted by the world as normal. Even with all of the aforementioned attributes, the truth still stands, and the truth is that God honors marriage. Many may say marriage is just a piece of paper, marriage is outdated, or you may as well be married since you do all of the above mentioned actions, etc., but the important thing to remember is that it's not about our opinions. I must repeat it's not about our opinions; it's about what God says. If you find yourself struggling with the foundational definition of being single, and I know some of you are, remember that we live by God's standards and not our own. We don't conform His standards to how we feel or what we think is right, we conform ourselves to what God has already said is right and thankfully, God never changes.

Contrary to what seems like popular belief, God didn't make a mistake in His standards of righteousness, nor are His mandates for marriage, abstinence, faith, patience and other principles time-bound. We say we believe in an all-knowing God but somehow some don't believe that He could set forth a standard of living that could apply to all generations. We want God's blessing laid out thousands of years ago to apply today but we want to bypass standards that were laid out at the same time. It is true that God's Word is written in different writing styles and time settings but we are not to pick and choose what we are going to follow based on how we feel or what we want to do. We are to be led by the Holy Spirit in the interpretation and understanding of God's Word. His Word truly stands the test of time and it would greatly benefit us to accept God and His Word for all that they are. Anything less would insinuate that we know more than God does. I know this can be a touchy or even controversial subject so before we move on to further delve into singleness; here are a few scriptures to read over and meditate on. As you read, allow the Holy Spirit to either confirm or convict your current views on God's Word and the principles therein. I encourage you to be open to His response either way.

In the beginning was the Word, and the Word was with God, and the Word was God. John 1:1(KJV)

Heaven and earth shall pass away: but my words shall not pass away. Mark 13:31(KJV)

Jesus Christ the same yesterday, and to day, and for ever. Hebrews 13:8 (KJV)

Now that we have a definition of single, let's look into the term purely single. When I would have conversations with people about my marital status I didn't feel as though just saying "I'm single" was enough to accurately describe the space I was in. Without thinking about it, I began to use the term purely single as I would discuss the subject with others. For me, purely single meant to be *unmarried, unattached from emotional and physical ties and romantically uninvolved with the opposite sex.* As I write this chapter in a purely single state, it means I'm not in a relationship with anyone nor am I involved in communicating with the opposite sex in a romantically inclined manner. My heart is completely undivided and free from the pull of anyone of the opposite sex. Keep in mind, this definition isn't meant to alienate anyone or cause division, it is meant only to highlight one aspect of being single that applies to a group of people including myself as I write this chapter.

My journey to the state of being purely single was a winding road but I'm glad for the time God has given me in this season. I was able to learn a lot of lessons that I might have otherwise missed out on if my attention was divided by a relationship. Growing up I wasn't allowed to date until I was 15 but as soon as I started dating it was a never- ending cycle from then until I was a junior in college. While I can count on less than one hand how many official boyfriends I have had, I was always what young adults like to call, "talking" to someone. There were only rare spaces where there wasn't someone I was talking to on the phone regularly and texting daily. I suffered with low self-esteem and I would admittedly talk to guys I had no interest in, just because I was so fascinated with someone being interested in me. I would later find out a lot of that "interest" was pretty superficial and it was more of a time-filler to avoid the truth of the real emptiness I felt. If we're honest, I'm sure lots of us have gone wrong in the area of relationships just because we want to be wanted.

I believe we're all built with an inner desire for companionship, and while earthly relationships are good, there's a place in our lives that can only be satisfied by God. That desire for wholeness is really the desire God placed in each one of us for a relationship with Him, but most of us try to fill it with other things (drugs, alcohol, sex, excessive partying, the love of a person, etc.) and wonder why we keep coming up short. That was me, and I tried to fill that yearning with people. I had a void, and even though I loved Jesus and experienced salvation as a child, I never let Him fill that void. I unknowingly tried to do it myself.

The void I was trying to fill came from facing a lot of rejection from a friendship standpoint. It honestly seemed as though every friend I had would walk away from me. Friendships with people I thought would be in my life forever just dissolved for what seemed like no apparent reason. As I mentioned earlier, I experienced salvation very early on. People would say I was different because I wasn't afraid to voice my belief in Jesus as my Savior. As I grew up in the Lord I didn't do things other kids my age would do. I stopped listening to a lot of secular music, I didn't watch certain movies, I didn't curse or go to the club and by the grace of God I remained a virgin. Subconsciously, I resented God a little bit that it seemed like I couldn't keep friendships because of my convictions. I was always "different" and truth be told I would much rather just fit in. I would eventually learn to embrace my difference because it's exactly what Christ followers are called to be, but for the time being, the sting of rejection would run rampant through my life for many years.

I wondered why I couldn't love God, live for Him and keep my friendships intact. It hurt so much and I would often cry at the burden of pure loneliness I felt at times. I could never understand why I had to be so alone. Because of this, my views of God and His love were restrained and a void of acceptance was left gaping open.

I have to digress quickly here for a moment because I feel it's important to note that in hindsight I realize that some people are only in your life for a season and you have to be ok with that. God will allow different relationships to dissolve because people are assigned to your life for different reasons. I want you to be careful to remember that every person that crosses your path is on assignment, whether that assignment is good or evil. I won't say that any of my friendships were evil but it doesn't mean that they served the greater purpose for my life. If I truly look at those friendships I know that those people, no matter how much I loved them, weren't meant to come on this part of the journey with me. We were on the same path for the time being but eventually the road diverged and we were led two different ways. God knew this would happen and He allowed that rejection or dissolution of the relationship to occur in order to ensure that I would be at this very place in this very moment. As you grow, and you should if you've really dedicated your life to Christ, God will provide you with exactly what you need when you need it. It's ok to release people and friendships as the Lord leads you.

Now back to the subject at hand. After ending a turbulent relationship with my last boyfriend I knew that I didn't want to continue operating in the same way in my life. It was only God that allowed the following sequence of events to reveal to me how I could move forward. I remember my senior year of college sitting in my dorm room scrolling through twitter when I read a simple tweet that said "God is so in love with you". It immediately captured my attention and I found myself reading that statement over and over. I had been a Christian just about all my life and never read anything quite like that. I had never really thought about the idea of God being in love with me. I knew He loved me but to know that He was *in love* with me meant something almost totally different than what I had conceptualized. Being in love was sort of a mystery for me. I had loved in relationships but never what I would consider being in love. I knew being in love was something serious, almost unfathomable, especially from God. That same day I came across a song called "How He Loves" by John Mark McMillan (1). I encourage you to listen to it and look up the lyrics if you don't know it. Something about that song rang truth in my spirit and it was like understanding something I had never understood before. I used to think of God's love as more of a one way street from Him to us, but according to what I now understood, He wanted our love as well. I wanted to be wanted by all these people and God wanted me. Not just loved me, but wanted me.

I can't even begin to explain how the combination of that tweet, that song and the inner work of the Holy Spirit began to open my mind to a new understanding of my relationship with God. I had a desire to go further and deeper in God than I ever had before. Perhaps if I took a leap of faith and truly believed God was in love with me then I would be able to find the love and acceptance I could never seem to find amongst the people in my life. There was honestly nowhere else but up from there, so it was worth a try. That night I prayed and told the Lord that I didn't want to experience the love of a spouse before I really felt what it was like to be in love with God. I wanted to experience His love. Not just know about it, not just talk about it, but experience it. I realized I had a void. There was no way I could call myself a Christian and not endeavor to understand God's love for me in a greater way. I was fed up with trying to make all these friendships and relationships work and ending up in the same place. I didn't just want Him to fill my voids, I wanted Him to fill me up so much that my whole life overflowed with Him; every word, every action, every thought.

I was tired of waiting around for life to get better so I made a decision to focus on God and cut off unnecessary relationships. During this time, several of what I considered my good friendships either ended or we naturally drifted apart. I was even more alone than where I had started but I know now that I needed that separation in order to be broken of my dependence on the presence of people. I began to read my bible more and just spend time talking to God. I had to face the fact that I had no one else to talk to and that's exactly how God began to heal me. For some of us, it takes a complete break down for us to see God for all of who He is. I became intentional about making time to worship, reading my bible and praying. These were daily choices to turn off the TV, finish my homework, and get off Facebook so that I could spend time with God. I didn't just wait for some free time to show up in my day, I made time. It was an everyday choice, even when I didn't really "feel" like it because I was tired of being empty and God was the only hope I had to becoming whole.

As I made that intention day after day for a while, I noticed one day while I was in class that I couldn't wait to get back to my dorm and talk to God. I once would feel highly disappointed when my phone wasn't buzzing with notifications, but I had found it was much more satisfying and much less stressful to talk to God about things rather than people. I looked forward to just talking to Him. It may sound crazy but it's true. It's really something quite amazing for someone who used to hate being alone to actually look forward to being alone so I could be with God! If you've ever truly been lonely you know what a testimony that is. I knew then that God had done what I asked Him to do the night I prayed that prayer. He had filled my voids and I was actually in love with Him.

Through that discovery, I found out that the love of a person would never satisfy me. I tried over and over to believe my last boyfriend really loved me but it just wasn't good enough. I knew that wasn't real love. There was always something missing for me. I thought perhaps over time he would change and love me like I wanted but several years went by and that didn't happen. Sometimes you have to just face the fact that no matter how much effort, time or emotion you put into a relationship, it's not meant to be. I held on to his potential instead of the reality that this relationship wasn't what I wanted. I thought I should hold on and make it work but God kept tugging on my heart. I knew for sure this wasn't a relationship God wanted me to be in but I found it so hard to let go of. Who wants to start a new relationship from scratch with someone in the future when you can just stay with the person you've known for years? I learned then not to stay in relationships for pure convenience.

I couldn't find it in myself to end the relationship so I decided to give this prayer a try that I had heard another young lady give a testimony about. That night I prayed that if God didn't want us to be together to have the young man break up with me. Sure enough a few days later he broke up with me. I don't even remember why. From that point on, I knew I wasn't supposed to be with him but I would go on to continue to talk and hang out with him as "friends" for about another 2 years before enough became truly enough and I cut it off completely. For the first year after the breakup, we remained really close. I called him my best friend but it was a romantic friendship at times. That was a mistake and if I could give any advice to anyone in this situation, you can't truly be just friends with someone you have feelings for. Don't play yourself, this was a ploy on my behalf to try to have my cake and eat it too. I was being somewhat obedient in not being in a relationship anymore but I did not set the boundaries necessary to make the relationship completely platonic.

By the second year, the friendship had become rocky. I would see sparks here and there of the love and support I needed but then he would disappoint me in some manner and we wouldn't talk for a while. Several times we would resolve to save this wonderful friendship we thought we had and the cycle would start over. After graduating college, I had to go out of the state for a month for training. He was supposed to come see me a couple of days before I left but he never made it. Part of me wanted to make excuses for it as usual, but it only takes a second to send a text and I knew I deserved at least that. I didn't hear anything from him until the day I was leaving town and that's when I let him know that our friendship had run its course and it was best we go our separate ways. The chances to honor my feelings had run out; enough was enough. I decided that was the last time I would subject myself to being disappointed by empty words and a complete disregard for my feelings. Through the understanding of God's love, my expectations for the people in my life had been raised. For the first time I didn't feel bad about having standards.

I'm not going to act like it was easy to let this all go, it was extremely hard. I struggled for a while but chose to remain completely disconnected until my emotions were officially unattached. It was a hard lesson learned and many disappointments would have been avoided if I just let go when God told me to. In fact, when I look back I see so many red signs of God letting me know that this relationship wasn't what he wanted for me in the first place. I never had peace about it. There's an inner turmoil when you know you are doing something you aren't supposed to do. If you're reading this and God has given you your own red signs, don't ignore them. It hurts to let go of anything you love but it hurts even more if you wait. You will save so much time and heartache if you obey God early.

Like a lot of us, I tried to tweak God's instructions and justify my disobedience instead of letting go completely. It was through the learning of God's love for me that I was able to understand my worth and why it was ok to let go of him. The important thing here is to never hold on to what God is telling you to let go of. Sometimes you have to let go of good to get God's best, especially on your journey to receiving God's promise.

I decided to endeavor to be purely single because it was only in this place that I could come to the understanding I have now of what it means to be genuinely in love with God. Over the past 2 years, God has taken me on a journey of understanding His love that I never could have imagined that night. More of my experiences will be shared in the coming pages of this book but in totality I could only describe myself now and myself that night in 2012 as two different people. My passion to help people experience God's love was ignited then and only burns brighter now because I know how His love healed me. It healed my low self-esteem, my broken heart, and my fear of rejection. He took all the broken pieces of an emotionally rocky childhood and adolescence and gave me hope. That healing allowed me to face the world with confidence in the God I said I believed in.

Many of us church folk, whether those that have grown up in church or have just been a part of the church world for a long time, can be numb to the real passion behind what we believe in. We hear so much that God loves us that we lose the depth and realness of what that actually means (Romans 8:38-39). I'm so grateful God loves me in spite of my many, many downfalls. His love truly lifts me. Is everyday perfect? Absolutely not. Do I still want to be married? Absolutely yes! But the understanding of God's love for us is the foundation for this topic of waiting on God so I wanted to make sure to expound on this point. It will be an extremely rough, lonely season of waiting if you don't know how much God loves you.

Being purely single has been an absolute blessing for me as it allowed me the time I needed to develop my love for God beyond just surface-level, generalized emotion. I do realize that God may not have for everyone's journey to be "purely single" at any point in their life; there are other paths God can use to get you from point A to point B. My main goal is for everyone to believe that it is possible to be in love with God, it's not just a church cliché. If you're in a relationship you have no peace about, let it go. If you're waiting for God to send some huge sign that it isn't meant to be, He's telling you right now with that uneasy feeling you have every time you think about that relationship. If God has not brought your spouse yet and you haven't really spent any time alone and undistracted then maybe you should consider a season of being purely single. Even if you're married, you may have some areas in your relationship with Christ that could use a little less distraction. Give God an opportunity to reveal Himself and His love to you like never before. This is essential to maximizing every season of life, including your seasons of waiting. That's what being purely single is all about, the life of an unmarried person with God at the center. It's never too late for any of us, no matter what our relationship status is, to refocus and reprioritize so that God is the center of our lives.

I have been crucified with Christ. It is no longer I who live, but Christ who lives in me. And the life I now live in the flesh I live by faith in the Son of God, who loved me and gave himself for me.
Galatians 2:20 (ESV)

2

The Balancing Act

Not that I speak in respect of want: for I have learned, in whatsoever state I am, therewith to be content.
Philippians 4:11(KJV)

As I mentioned in the Purely Single chapter, I absolutely want to be married one day. I think it's important to talk about this because a lot of people seem timid to admit what they want. I believe it should be our goal to be content but we can reach that without having to deny what we desire. You are not "thirsty" if you want to be married one day and you will find it much easier to be content if you embrace the desire rather than try to separate yourself as far as possible from it. God created marriage, and most likely if you have a desire for it then it's there because God plans to fulfill it. The challenging part is balancing the desires you have with being content.

To be content means to be pleased and satisfied (2). From this standpoint it's pretty clear that just the desire for something in itself doesn't mean that you cannot be satisfied with either being single or being in whatever state you are in before you receive something from God. The key here is to analyze WHY you desire this thing. If you're single, take a few minutes to think about why you want to be married before you continue reading. If it's something else that you want, you can think about why you desire that as well.

If the thought of marriage brings to mind romantic outings, public displays of affection, and someone to call your own, then that desire is for selfish gain and therefore not glorifying to God. I know we see these images all over our televisions, internet, magazines and so much more but the purpose of marriage is not just to fulfill your romantic desires. In the same way, God's fulfillment of your prayers isn't just to feed your ego or make you wealthy and famous. Let's take a look at Adam and Eve to see if we can better understand why God brings two people together and use the example of marriage as a testament of God's intentions in blessing you.

And the LORD God took the man, and put him into the garden of Eden to dress it and to keep it. [16] And the LORD God commanded the man, saying, Of every tree of the garden thou mayest freely eat: [17] But of the tree of the knowledge of good and evil, thou shalt not eat of it: for in the day that thou eatest thereof thou shalt surely die. [18] And the LORD God said, It is not good that the man should be alone; I will make him an help meet for him.
Genesis 2:15-18 (KJV)

The Lord God said that He made Eve to help Adam. Adam was given an assignment to keep the Garden of Eden and Eve was there to help him complete that assignment. God didn't say Adam needed romance or someone to love and complete him; he needed help carrying out God's instructions. Now don't get me wrong, love should surely be a part of your marriage but shifting our perspective will help us in making sure our desires are pleasing to God and not a hindrance to our contentment. God does everything with purpose so if you focus on the purpose of marriage then you may have an easier time understanding how God works and feel less inclined to rush Him. Everything that we do should be to glorify God, in fact let's see some proof of that in the Word.

Whether therefore ye eat, or drink, or whatsoever ye do, do all to the glory of God
1 Corinthians 10:31(KJV)

All of us should want our lives to bring glory to God. In essence, that's what we are here to do. So let's be honest here, have we even taken the time to consider what purpose our marriage will serve in the kingdom of God? Have we thought about the opportunities to follow our God-given instructions and fulfill the great commission (Matthew 28:19-20) through that blessing we're asking for? Have we even dedicated ourselves to figuring out God's purpose for us as an individual? Most of us, me included, tend to be selfish in this regard. We want something simply because we want it, not because of anything else or any greater purpose. Whether you've discovered it already or not, God always has purpose in mind. There's nothing you can think of that He created that doesn't serve a purpose. Let's just use the human body as an example. Most of us take something as simple as finger nails for granted. For women, they're often nifty accessories that we decorate but we don't keep the purpose of them at the forefront of our minds. If you just take a moment to think about it, there are a lot of everyday tasks we would be unable to accomplish as easily without them. Simple things like picking up tiny objects or scratching that annoying itch would be nearly impossible. We don't readily think about their purpose but we need them. Fortunately for us, even when we aren't thinking about purpose, God is. Marriage, children, and everything else have a purpose for you in the correct time and correct season and understanding this will help move you towards a more satisfying life.

As long as your desires line up with God's will then He will fulfill it at the appointed time, but it isn't His will for you to be tormented about it. For example, if your desire for marriage has taken over every waking moment of your life and is eating you up inside as you wait for your spouse then there's something wrong. God is NOT a tormentor, His plans for you are good not evil (Jeremiah 29:11). Obviously, it's important to put this desire in the proper context so that it doesn't overwhelm you or cause you to stumble. Your future marriage is so important to God that He won't just lay it before you for no reason at all. This is why many teach that single people should get busy working for the Lord during this season. If you aren't taking steps to fulfill your purpose why would He provide you with any help? In the same notion, I don't believe that being busy working for the Lord means that you will never think about receiving what it is that you want from God. Perhaps that works for some people but I can testify for myself that it didn't happen to me. I served in the church, held a full time job, and worked on graduate studies but marriage still ran across my mind. This is where our mindset becomes just that much more important. We have to remain centered on God and not have God on the outskirts of everything else in our lives. If at any time our thoughts deviate from using every blessing to glorify God, it is our responsibility to check ourselves and bring our thoughts back into alignment.

You should have come to the realization now that it isn't the desire for something from God that's the issue; it's why we desire it. It is totally possible to be a satisfied single even while desiring to be married in the future. I believe a shift in focus from us to God is monumental in coming to a place of peace within your season of waiting. Let's take a moment to meditate on another verse that may help tremendously in finally arriving to the much desired place of contentment.

To every thing there is a season, and a time to every purpose under the heaven:
Ecclesiastes 3:1 (KJV)

My next piece of Godly wisdom as it pertains to keeping the desire for marriage and other blessings in check is to remember that life works in seasons. Every season has a beginning and an end. God has already purposed a specific time period in your life to be single and a specific time period to be married. Your current relationship status is no surprise to Him and no matter what you do, it won't change what He has already purposed. God's timing is perfect. It may not always seem that way, but we serve a sovereign God. He divinely orchestrates our lives such that all things work together for the good of those that love Him and are called according to His purpose (Romans 8:28). To trust God during this time means to rely on the fact that He has the ability to select the best time and speed to move you out of your current state and accomplish His will in your life.

We've talked a lot about finding that balance between contentment and desire but as in the case of real balances, it is always a possibility to lean too far to one side or the other. Continuing in the same example, we know going too far into the desire for marriage will lead to a lot of unnecessary stress, more susceptibility to making the wrong decisions and undoubtedly some disappointments. For example, I know of many women who wanted to be married so bad that they made the wrong choice in boyfriends and husbands. They swear up and down God told or showed them this man was the one and then once in the relationship they realized there was a good possibility that they may have heard God wrong. You see, even though God speaks to us, we have our own filters that we take His words through. Our fleshly desires, past experiences and personal perceptions can cause us to hear God incorrectly or twist His words to mean something they do not; especially when it's something we really want. I encourage everyone, no matter what marital status or what you're thinking God told you, to not allow any desire to be so strong that it clouds your ability to hear God clearly. Our flesh is always against God (Galatians 5:17) so we have to be extra careful that we are not being led astray by our own desires. Try every spirit (1 John 4:1), ask God for confirmations and be sure that you have God's instructions before you make decisions.

On the other end of the spectrum, I experienced a season in my life where I was too content. I was about a year out from my dorm room prayer I talked about earlier in the book where I had told God I wanted to experience what it was like to be in love with Him. I had also graduated from college and moved out on my own for the first time. I was so comfortable being single that I actually started questioning if I really wanted to get married one day. The loss of my new found freedom and the peace of not having to deal with the issues of a relationship just didn't seem worth it. Not only that, I became very possessive. God blessed me with my own home and the ability to buy everything in it and all of it was mine and mine alone. I couldn't really find it in myself to want to share. It was all about me during this time in my life, and as much as I hate to admit it, it felt ridiculously great.

During this time, God took me through a trust test to reel me back in to reality. He told me to give a specific amount of money to my church at the time. *As a disclaimer, I knew this was God's instruction and I was not pressured by any outside force to give any amount of money to the church. Be prayerfully led by God when giving, not by man.* I fought it as long as I could but He just kept pressing it on me until I couldn't ignore it anymore. It also "just so happened" that at the time we were learning about being stewards of God's resources on this Earth and not owners. This was huge for me, like so huge I worried about being able to pay my bills if I gave this amount of money. I even questioned if God would really make me do such a thing and tried to talk myself out of it. There was no escaping. I knew in my heart what He wanted me to do. It was really hard but I decided to trust God and give the money. I told God I trusted Him, wrote the check and sowed the seed.

That moment changed my life forever. I learned that what's mine is not mine, it's His. The Earth is the Lord's and the fullness thereof (Psalm 24:1). He is so gracious to allow us all these freedoms and then we take and hoard them for ourselves. I can't stake claim on anything I have, it all belongs to Him. As I talked about extensively at the beginning of this chapter, everything should be used for His glory. I wasn't focused on His glory at all, I was focused on myself. There are extremes to contentment that we should be careful to avoid because they are detrimental to our spiritual growth. And for those that may be wondering, I'll be completely honest here, no the test didn't end when I put the check in the bucket. I continued to be tested on where my trust lay for several months, but the Lord did provide for me in different ways after I sowed that seed.

Besides learning about how selfish I had become in my contentment, I learned that going too far into contentment can become a guard against what God may be trying to give to us. If I would have stayed in that mode I probably would have missed a lot of blessings because I was too focused on where I was right then. My heart became guarded because I didn't want to engage in a relationship and lose the good I thought I had going on as a single. I was very successful according to most standards and to top it all off I had peace. I spent a lot of time in a relationship with someone I had no peace about so this feeling was something I for sure didn't want to give up. I didn't want for anything and bringing a man in seemed to be a downgrade. I was ok staying just the way I was. This is the wrong mindset and it is sometimes mistaken as the goal of contentment. You don't want to be so content in your current situation that you become stagnant. You should never be so focused on where you are that you stop pressing forward.

Anything God brings to your life is to enhance, not to take you backwards. Be open to change because it's inevitable and necessary for growth. Trust me it's better to avoid the walls going up than have God knock them down. The true balance is being grateful for where you are while having a continued expectation to receive even more of God's promised blessings in the days to come. Once you find that balance in your life you'll see why this passage Paul writes in 1st Timothy is so true.

But godliness with contentment is great gain.
1 Timothy 6:6 (KJV)

3

The Danger of Discontentment

And the mixt multitude that was among them fell a lusting: and the children of Israel also wept again, and said, Who shall give us flesh to eat? [5] We remember the fish, which we did eat in Egypt freely; the cucumbers, and the melons, and the leeks, and the onions, and the garlick: [6] But now our soul is dried away: there is nothing at all, beside this manna, before our eyes.
Numbers 11:4-6 (KJV)

The children of Israel had been delivered from the hands of the Egyptians by God through Moses when we find them in Numbers Chapter 11. As they were traveling to their promised land, God provided them with all their needs. They had food, clothes, shelter and a mighty God leading them every step of the way. It is here the Bible notes something very significant that many people probably look over. In fact, I looked over it for years until the Lord brought it to my attention in February 2014. That significant element is found in Numbers 11 verse 4 where it says that a mixed multitude of people were with the children of Israel in their journey. We see the mixed multitude mentioned in Exodus 12 as well as Numbers 11.

And the mixt multitude that was among them fell a lusting: and the children of Israel also wept again, and said, Who shall give us flesh to eat?
Number 11:4 (KJV)

And a mixed multitude went up also with them; and flocks, and herds, even very much cattle.
Exodus 12:38 (KJV)

There are a couple of theories about who this mixt multitude was but we can surmise they were not full blood Israelites since they are listed separately. But something serious happens with this mixt multitude; they began to lust, or desire something they couldn't have. Consequently, their lust rubbed off on the Israelites and they began to complain about not having the food they once had in slavery in Egypt. The lust of the outsiders brought it to the attention of the Israelites that they were seemingly missing something. Discontentment is defined as the restless desire or craving for something one does not have (3). The feeling of discontentment doesn't happen overnight. It is a gradual process that starts long before you may experience the emotions that come along with it. Dissatisfaction, like what we see displayed here with the Israelites, is the first step in the process towards discontentment.

The outsiders that travelled out of Egypt seemed to have a great memory of where they had come from, but they remembered the wrong thing. While their focus should have been on what God had done for the Israelites in delivering them from Pharaoh, they were thinking about something as minute as a lack of food choice. We can judge the Israelites here unfairly but I know all of us have had the experience of people who on the surface appear to care about you but have an opinion about your life that isn't encouraging at all. If you're in school, they want to know when you're graduating. If you graduated, they want to know when you're getting married. If you're married, they want to know when you're going to have children. It's so easy to let people make you discontent and the Israelites failed this test. They were fine eating manna until someone else made it seem like they were lacking something. I'm sure we can all relate to the Israelites here. We were just fine until someone reminded us how long we've been single, or how long we've been praying for that breakthrough. In truth, the Israelites lacked nothing. We serve a God that knows our needs (Matthew 6:8) so if they needed more, He would have provided it. Contentment is all in a mindset. Be sure to guard your boundaries of influence and make sure someone else's lust isn't pulling you astray.

The Israelites felt dissatisfaction as they compared their present situation to their past. They mistakenly allowed the mixed multitude to affect their thinking and cause them to desire enslavement over freedom. Instead of focusing on the miraculous things the Lord had done for them, their attention was drawn to their lack. Just think, we read and marvel at the Lord bringing the plagues on Egypt and splitting the red sea and the people that were there actually experiencing it allowed themselves to be distracted over food. They were the promised people, how could they let people without a promise have such influence over them? It is much the same for us now. Instead of focusing on the blessing of what we have, we're distraught over what we don't have. While slavery was harsh, they had become accustomed to it and bondage was their comfort zone. For most of us, the greatest moves of God occur outside of our comfort zone. It's unfortunate that the children of Israel didn't take the time to see that. Even though they had left Egypt, it would take a long time to remove their slave mentality.

The next stage of the process to discontentment is discouragement. We find the children of Israel often discouraged during their journey to the promise land. Once you become dissatisfied in your journey to promise, discouragement is not far behind. God will often move you out of your comfort zone to take you into the next level of life, but of course in any movement there is a transition period. The transition period can be scary and your faith is often tested here, but it is not the time to start thinking negatively about what God is doing. Soon after the children of Israel left Egypt they felt their first moment of discomfort with Pharaoh on their tails and immediately became discouraged.

And when Pharaoh drew nigh, the children of Israel lifted up their eyes, and, behold, the Egyptians marched after them; and they were sore afraid: and the children of Israel cried out unto the LORD.[11] And they said unto Moses, Because there were no graves in Egypt, hast thou taken us away to die in the wilderness? Wherefore hast thou dealt thus with us, to carry us forth out of Egypt?[12] Is not this the word that we did tell thee in

Egypt, saying, Let us alone, that we may serve the
Egyptians? For it had been better for us to serve the
Egyptians, than that we should die in the wilderness.
Exodus 14:10-12 (KJV)

Now surely the children of Israel had to know that the same God who delivered them from Pharaoh would not turn around and allow them to die at the hands of him. It sounds so easy to believe, but in the midst of your transition periods how do you react? We may ask God for something and then as soon as a greater level of trust and responsibility is required, we renege on our request. We are often no different than the Israelites, but we have a tendency to judge them very harshly.

How many of us would rather stay in our comfort zone than go through a few tests to get to our promise? I know for me, for a short while after coming out of my season of being too content, I wanted to go back. Why be open to relationship and vulnerability when I can be single and protected from the possibility of being hurt? For sure I would not be where I am today in any area of life if I knew beforehand what I would go through to get here. In the transition, a true relationship with God will enable you to keep the faith. For when you know your God, you know He will never leave you. You know that no matter how you feel, He is with you (Deuteronomy 31:6). We are not always prepared for where God is taking us but it is during the transition period that He fixes this disparity. Do not become discouraged, trust Him no matter what.

Once you come to the point of discouragement you easily slip into discontentment, but unfortunately it doesn't stop there. You begin to strongly desire what you do not have and then wind up in disbelief. You don't have confidence in God's ability to do what He has promised so you cop out and settle for less. Two tribes in the children of Israel allowed disbelief to affect their promise; we find their story in Numbers Chapter 32.

Now the children of Reuben and the children of Gad had a very great multitude of cattle: and when they saw the land of Jazer, and the land of Gilead, that, behold, the place was a place for cattle;² The children of Gad and the children of Reuben came and spake unto Moses, and to Eleazar the priest, and unto the princes of the congregation, saying,³ Ataroth, and Dibon, and Jazer, and Nimrah, and Heshbon, and Elealeh, and Shebam, and Nebo, and Beon,⁴ Even the country which the LORD smote before the congregation of Israel, is a land for cattle, and thy servants have cattle:⁵ Wherefore, said they, if we have found grace in thy sight, let this land be given unto thy servants for a possession, and bring us not over Jordan.⁶ And Moses said unto the children of Gad and to the children of

Reuben, Shall your brethren go to war, and shall ye sit here?[7] And wherefore discourage ye the heart of the children of Israel from going over into the land which the LORD hath given them?
Numbers 32:1-7(KJV)

The children of Israel had a land flowing with milk and honey that the Lord had already promised to give them, but upon seeing just enough land for their families and cattle, the tribes of Reuben and Gad decided to settle. They settled for just enough instead of the abundance God had promised. Not only that, we can note here that every decision we make has an effect on other people. Moses chastised the two tribes because their settling was about more than just them; it was a discouragement for the other tribes that had to keep going. Who will be affected if you decide to settle before you reach God's promise?

Oftentimes what God has promised is beyond our capacity to comprehend so we operate in fear and take what we can get. It's much easier to settle for what's in front of you than to keep pressing and believe God for what you don't see. How many of us abort our promise process by settling for mediocrity? We may feel we don't deserve any great promises or find it too risky to believe God for greatness, so we stop where we are, cut our losses and throw in the towel. We'll take just enough, even though God has promised more than enough.

Discontentment leads to disbelief, which causes us to miss out on the fulfillment of God's blessings. I'll be the first to admit that I often have to remind myself that I can expect to see God's goodness in this Earth. For some reason we think all the greatness for a believer is in heaven and whatever we get on Earth is just what it is (Psalm 27:13). We'll settle for being sickly, broke, or in an unhealthy relationship because we really don't trust God for better. It must truly pain God to see His children so satisfied with living below our birth right. Don't allow the process of discontentment to lead to disbelief and cause you to settle. I want to encourage you. God will do exactly what He said He will do; He's just waiting on you to believe that.

Lastly, the disbelief that comes from the process of discontentment leads to disobedience. We want what we can't have and don't believe God will give us what we want so we go against God's will to try to get it ourselves. I see this happen a lot with single people who desire marriage. They aren't happy single and they don't believe God will send them the mate they desire so they sin and scheme to try to find a mate themselves. They'll dress and talk provocatively, search for attention on social media and give their bodies to people who aren't their spouse all in the name of finding and keeping love. We   disregard

God's instructions and do it our own way because we lack faith, patience and self-control. Moses decided to disregard God's instructions in the desert of Zin when there was no water and the children of Israel were thirsty. Let's pick up with Moses in Numbers Chapter 20.

And the LORD spake unto Moses, saying,[8] Take the rod, and gather thou the assembly together, thou, and Aaron thy brother, and speak ye unto the rock before their eyes; and it shall give forth his water, and thou shalt bring forth to them water out of the rock: so thou shalt give the congregation and their beasts drink.[9] And Moses took the rod from before the LORD, as he commanded him.[10] And Moses and Aaron gathered the congregation together before the rock, and he said unto them, Hear now, ye rebels; must we fetch you water out of this rock?[11] And Moses lifted up his hand, and with his rod he smote the rock twice: and the water came out abundantly, and the congregation drank, and their beasts also.[12] And the LORD spake unto Moses and Aaron, Because ye believed me not, to sanctify me in the eyes of the children of Israel, therefore ye shall not bring this congregation into the land which I have given them.
Numbers 20:7-12(KJV)

It's interesting here that although Moses and Aaron did not follow God's instructions, He says that they are punished because of their disbelief, not their disobedience. Disobedience is the result of disbelief. When you truly do not believe that something will happen with God, you will find it acceptable to do it your own way and not God's way. That is the definition of disobedience. It goes deeper than just not doing what you are told. If you find yourself in constant rebellion against authority whether that be God, your parents, your spouse, law enforcement, or anything else, you need to examine the root of that disobedience. It's beyond important to catch the root of disbelief BEFORE it causes you to step outside of the will of God. Outside of His will you will find consequences, inside of it is protection. When you trust God, you will do what He says to do. In fact, if you *love* God you will do what He says to do. We show God we love Him when we are obedient.

If ye love me, keep my commandments.
John 14:15(KJV)

Ultimately, discontentment means that you are not submissive to the will of God. You don't trust Him, His timing or His provision and you think you are in need of something He hasn't given you. This is a dangerous way to live, but many people operate with this thought process every day. We have got to learn how to recognize the signs of the process of discontentment so it doesn't hinder our spiritual growth. I know we went over a lot of different words so here is a quick visual of what the process of discontentment looks like.

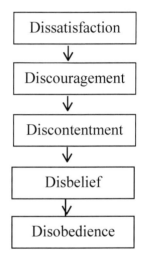

Dissatisfaction
↓
Discouragement
↓
Discontentment
↓
Disbelief
↓
Disobedience

Knowing this process of discontentment and just how far it can go is so important because it can lead to ramifications far beyond what you can imagine. It can cloud our judgment and ultimately change the course of our lives forever. While you're waiting and walking your journey to promise, you can't afford to have anything distract you or take you off the path. Both outside and inside influences will try to discourage you during this time but stay focused and remember all that God has done for you. Check your feelings of dissatisfaction and discouragement so they do not grow into discontentment and later lead to disobedience. Thankfully, you do not have to depend on yourself to guard against discontentment. The Holy Spirit is our helper and we should lean to Him to help us navigate the decisions of life. He will lead and guide us into all truth (John 16:13).

4

The Thief of Comparison

And be not conformed to this world: but be ye transformed by the renewing of your mind, that ye may prove what is that good, and acceptable, and perfect, will of God.
Romans 12:2 (KJV)

A lot of our discontentment stems from looking outside of God to see what life should be like and then measuring ourselves to that standard. I strongly believe that there are a lot of ways we hinder God greatly in our lives, and one of those things is our engagement in the activity of comparison. When we compare, we consider something in respect to something else and not as an individual component. Instead of evaluating a subject based on its inherent worth and singular characteristics, we assign value based on popularity or the degree in which the subject is similar to something else. For example, a person may want to buy a certain shoe because it's what everyone else is wearing instead of the fact that they just like the shoe itself. We compare things every day like prices and clothes but a problem arises when we allow that same mindset to drift into our personal lives. For believers, I find that problems arise both when we compare ourselves to the world and when we compare ourselves to other people.

I see a lot of people leading their lives based on what they are "supposed" to do in society's norms. For example, you're "supposed" to go to college after high school; you're "supposed" to get married sometime after college and much more. If you spend too much time in the world and not enough time in the Word, you will begin to think that you have to fit into society's mold. For those that may be unclear on what I mean by the term

43

"the world", I mean the segment of people that do not believe in Jesus as their Lord and Savior. We generally view people in an all-inclusive manner, but there is a difference between those who follow Jesus and those who choose to follow other beliefs. God made you for the purpose of doing something very specific on this Earth for His glory. You can't envision your life based on what other people have done and what other people will think because you will completely lose your individuality. To lose your identity by shaping your life to the curve of society is such a terrible devaluation.

There is great value in being different from the world, and Satan would love for you to fit in and fail to realize how important your contribution is to the Kingdom of God. The enemy is a thief (John 10:10) and to steal your identity in Christ is a surefire way to hinder you from progressing in God's will. You don't want to open yourself up to becoming dissatisfied with your life because it isn't going in the way you previously planned even though you never consulted with God when you made that life plan. There is a great danger in feeling as though you can guide your own life and make your decisions contingent upon the trends of society.

There is a way which seems right to a man and appears straight before him, but at the end of it is the way of death.
Proverbs 14:12 (AMP)

Though the plan you made without consulting God seems great and feasible, if it isn't what God has planned for you then it leads to destruction. I want to inspire a new generation of people that aren't guided by what they are supposed to do in their life according to society but rather by the Holy Spirit who promises to lead and guide us into the truth (John 16:13). God's plan for you is not a cookie cutter fit into a predisposed mold. You are unique. Your life was designed with you in mind and you need to seek God for His instructions. When speaking to Jeremiah, God says before Jeremiah was placed into His mother's womb He had purposed him for what He would accomplish in this Earth.

Before I formed thee in the belly I knew thee; and before thou camest forth out of the womb I sanctified thee, and I ordained thee a prophet unto the nations.
Jeremiah 1:5 (KJV)

To live this life and never fulfill the purpose God had set out for you is a travesty. He is the Creator of the universe, He knows much better than you do how to govern your life. Don't be afraid to ask God for direction, and then, most importantly, wait until He gives it. I believe He delights when we seek Him instead of seeking a worldly solution. Imagine you have a child that's learning how to ride a bike. Would you rather them go ask a stranger to teach them? Or come to you, their loving parent, to ask for help? He may very well want you to attend college after high school, get married before 30, have all your kids before 40 and retire at 60 but do that because God wants you to and not because you felt you were supposed to because of everyone else.

I know societal pressures are not easy to deal with and it sounds much easier said than done. I spent a lot of my early years doing things because I thought I had to. I never sought God for direction in my decisions. To be honest, I didn't recognize that as an essential part of the Christian life until I was well into college. I decided to major in engineering my senior year of high school based on what other people told me I should do. I was one of those children that wanted to be everything when I grew up, a nurse, teacher, writer, you name it. By the time I was a junior in high school, I didn't have any idea what I wanted to be and it seemed that everyone wanted to know what I was going to major in. It was an immense amount of pressure to be under. I felt like I had to live up to everyone's expectations, but I honestly didn't know what I wanted to do. I did well in math and science in school and I was told I would make a lot of money as an engineer so I did some preliminary research and just latched onto it. I began telling everyone I would major in engineering and the pressure was temporarily relieved.

Around my sophomore year of college the pressure was back. I realized I really didn't want to be an engineer. I had taken quite a few classes in my field already and I just wasn't into it. Only a small bit of the information I was learning was actually interesting to me and I just knew I didn't want to do this for the rest of my life. I wanted more for my life than to wake up and dread going to work every day. I learned through a summer job at a preschool and working with the youth at my church that I had a passion for children and teens. I really wanted to do something to help people succeed both spiritually and naturally, but I still wasn't exactly sure what I could do. Despite my desire to do something else, 2 years' worth of engineering related course credits loomed over me. A switch of majors meant at least a year of additional time in undergrad. I wasn't too fond of that option so I decided to tough it out and finish the engineering degree in the 4 years I had planned on.

Now I'm so thankful we serve a God that uses everything for our good. I made decisions for superficial reasons, like most young people do, but He still used that time to help me grow. That time wasn't wasted and it allowed me to be where I am today. But what if I had sought the Lord about what to major in instead of only listening to the people around me? How much time and frustration would I have saved? I know we all have those areas in our lives where we wish we would have sought God for His direction beforehand. God has a plan for us and we will avoid so much unnecessary trouble if we seek His plan instead of looking for answers outside of Him. If you're in a situation where you feel pressured to make a decision or live up to the world's standards, just think of all the time and heartache you will save if you seek God. Wise counsel is great, but at the end of the day the greatest counsel is that of the Lord. Don't allow comparison to steal your time or your future by caving under society's pressures and ignoring the desires God has placed within you.

It is extremely dangerous for a believer to compare themselves to the world and their way of doing things. We stop standing out and begin to adapt to the darkness of the world, slowly dimming our light and inhibiting the light of Christ from shining through us. This may be done either unknowingly or knowingly, but the result is the same either way. When we accept Jesus into our hearts and choose to live for Him, we choose a life that doesn't resemble the masses. Our standard is set forth in the Word of God and we have to be aware that we can't look at the world as an example for how we should conduct our lives. In a world where reality TV and reality stars reign, we have developed a skewed view of what the Believer's reality should be. We start to think about things from the viewpoint of what "everybody else" does instead of what's right biblically. Paul commands us not to acclimate ourselves to the world and to remain separated from the way they conduct their lives and affairs because the way of the world is not of God. You cannot be in the world and in God at the same time, or love the things of the world and claim to love God. This is made clear in several scriptures in the Word of God. The world is not your place of counsel nor should it be a place of comparison.

Ye adulterers and adulteresses, know ye not that the friendship of the world is enmity with God? whosoever therefore will be a friend of the world is the enemy of God.
James 4:4(KJV)

Love not the world, neither the things that are in the world. If any man love the world, the love of the Father is not in him.[16] For all that is in the world, the lust of the flesh, and the lust of the eyes, and the pride of life, is not of the Father, but is of the world.
1 John 2:15-16 (KJV)

Unfortunately, outside forces are not the only thing that will be exerting pressure on you to conform. We put ourselves in a similar predicament when we choose to compare ourselves to other people. I had a major stronghold in this area of my life for many years because of the struggle of low self-esteem. I was never good enough in the eyes of those around me so I succumbed to that belief myself. I wasn't often uplifted or celebrated for being who I was. My personality and physical characteristics were talked of negatively by loved ones and others my age so I didn't want to be me. I had been told to my face by a loved one that I was ugly, fat and didn't belong here. I held a strong face in the midst of verbal sometimes physical attack but it broke me on the inside. I was a verbal punching bag for many years, the chosen recipient of someone else's anger.

On top of that, I went to a predominantly Caucasian school and faced a few racial situations of children who saw me differently because of my skin color and made hurtful comments. The negative comments about my personality made it even worse. I wasn't outgoing and talkative, I was shy and quiet. This was partly due to the low self-esteem but mostly because that really was my personality. Everyone wanted me to talk more, be more energetic, or be more like another person they would so kindly name and describe in detail for me. I was faced with a constant barrage of people telling me I should be something other than what I was.

I tried so hard to conform to how others thought I should be and I failed every time. I would talk more and people still said I was quiet. I would be friendlier and people still said I was shy. I would work out hard and compete in sports and then they would say I was too muscular. It was a never-ending sequence of just not good enough. I became extremely self-conscious and overly critical of myself. I looked in the mirror and didn't see anything I liked. I had such a poor body image that what I saw back then in the mirror was completely different from reality. I couldn't change, no matter how hard I tried, so I disliked myself and was mad at God for making me this way.

And so began a vicious cycle of self-degradation and comparison to other people. I would look at other women day in and day out and wish I was them. I wanted her hair, her eyes, their personality and all the other things I felt I was lacking. There was never a day where I wasn't looking at another person and wanting what they had. I measured my life, my body, and my personality to what everyone else had and what everyone else viewed as good. If 115 pounds was the right size, I was the wrong size. If talkative and energetic was the right personality, then I had the wrong one. I envied other women and was extremely hard on myself. I prayed fervently for God to change me but He didn't. I was who I was and it wasn't until after I understood God's love for me that I began to accept the way He made me.

I now cringe at the time I spent wanting to be anything other than me. I look back at old pictures and am saddened by how I was so concerned with what I wasn't that I didn't enjoy what I was. In fact, I've spent the last couple of years trying to get back to the way I looked then! I understand now that there isn't one way of being that is correct and one that is wrong. We are not all made with Type A personalities, nor are we all size 2s and that's perfectly ok. God made everyone different because we all have different tasks to fulfill. Unfortunately, I didn't realize that. I thought there was something wrong with the way I was instead of focusing on all that was right. While there was a need to break out of my shell more in order to speak up for myself, there was nothing wrong with having a more reserved temperament.

Although the revelation of God's love for me changed my perspective, it's still a day to day decision to accept who I am. If a negative, self-defeating thought creeps up, I cancel it and refuse to let it stay. There will probably always be things I want to change but now when I look in the mirror I find things that I like about myself and focus on that. I also quote this scripture in Psalms to myself constantly.

I praise you, for I am fearfully and wonderfully made.
Wonderful are your works; my soul knows it very well.
Psalm 139:14 (ESV)

When I think in terms of purpose, I know God made me this way for a reason. I had to be exactly how He made me in order to fulfill His purpose for me on Earth. When you think this way, you tend to be more thankful for your portion. While I'm comparing myself to someone else, I don't know what that person had to do to get where they are. We always see the end result or the outside appearance and focus on that, not ever knowing the process that happened in order to bring them there. When I think of just myself I know that my struggles are nothing to envy. Furthermore, in the age of social media we live in, a couple of pictures on Facebook and Instagram are not typically an accurate depiction of what a person is really going through. Don't use social media as a measurement of someone's life.

In totality, your walk was foreordained by the God of the universe and He desires for you to focus on YOU and not everyone else's life. When you spend time focused on the wrong thing, you lose sight of your own goals and all the wonderful things God is doing in your life. There is a quote that sums up the importance of examining this subject matter that has been contributed to President Theodore Roosevelt; it says "comparison is the thief of joy". I couldn't agree more with this sentiment. I lost years of my life comparing myself to the world and to others and I missed out on celebrating the goodness of God during that time. The Bible says in Nehemiah 8:10 that the joy of the Lord is our strength. How much more then should we guard that joy with all we have? We cannot allow comparison to strip us of the strength we need to endure this life. Don't allow comparison to steal any time, any energy or any joy from you. Make a commitment to focus on you and never measure yourself against anything but God's standards. You are fearfully and wonderfully made (Psalm 139:14), the apple of your Father's eye (Psalm 17:8) and chosen to live a life set a part for His glory (1 Peter 2:9).

5

Weeds

Wherefore seeing we also are compassed about with so great a cloud of witnesses, let us lay aside every weight, and the sin which doth so easily beset us, and let us run with patience the race that is set before us.
Hebrews 12:1 (KJV)

Even in your best intentions to live righteously, situations, hurts, failures and disappointments can stack up in our lives and weigh us down. We internalize all that happens to us and never truly give it over to God, causing our spirits to become heavy and tired. We don't have the motivation to keep pushing, we give up easily and we're stuck wondering why it seems as though our life isn't moving forward. Once we get our mindset right, we have to also analyze the other forces that can seemingly hold us back. We think because we've swept something under the rug or chose to ignore it that we've let go of the things in life that hurt us, but God desires your complete freedom. You can't move any further in your walk with Christ if you are being weighed down.

Weight is not sin, as we see them listed separately in Hebrews 12:1, but it is something that is a serious detriment to your spiritual walk. God is so gracious that He won't take from us what we haven't given to Him. We must choose to lay aside these weights in order to walk in the fullness of God's calling and purpose for our lives. God has called us to greater but there are some things He wants you to know that you have to let go of. I thought that I had completely let go of the past but God took me on a journey in December 2013 that uncovered the root of a serious problem.

That December, I was at a point in my life where I was afraid of creating new relationships. I had been hurt by friendships and relationships in the past, but I had taken the time to heal and I knew it was time to move on. It sounded so simple, and it probably should have been exciting to start afresh, but the truth is I was doubtful. I was scared to create new relationships with people because of my past experiences. I had forgiven those who hurt me but I was fearful of the reality of having to open myself back up again. As I prayed, the Holy Spirit brought me to 1 John 4:18.

There is no fear in love; but perfect love casteth out fear: because fear hath torment. He that feareth is not made perfect in love.
1 John 4:18 (KJV)

I knew that God was telling me He didn't want me to be fearful but I still wasn't sure why I wasn't able to shake this fear of commitment and vulnerability. I had prayed and asked the Lord to help me in this area but I was left wondering how I could overcome this relational fear. The next day my daily bible verse came up and it was John 15:8. I had read this verse many times but a particular element stuck out to me that never stuck out before.

Herein is my Father glorified, that ye bear much fruit; so shall ye be my disciples
John 15:8 (KJV)

The word that stood out to me in John 15:8 was 'much'. Jesus had actually put a quantity on the fruit that we were to bear in order to bring God glory. There is detail there that's important for us to analyze. Think about it. When a tree bears only a little bit of fruit it can easily go both unnoticed and unrecognized. When a tree has an abundance of fruit, it is clearly visible and it is easily identified as to what kind of tree it is. It is the same with us today as it relates to our Christian walk. When we bear the fruit of the Spirit in abundance, people can't help but acknowledge who our God is and see how He has blessed us. If we read up a few verses we can delve even further into how our fruit is grown and maintained.

I am the true vine, and my Father is the husbandman.[2] Every branch in me that beareth not fruit he taketh away: and every branch that beareth fruit, he purgeth it, that it may bring forth more fruit.
John 15:1-2 (KJV)

The Word of God says that the Lord is the one who cultivates us and we grow through our attachment to Jesus as the vine. If we attach to Jesus but do not bear fruit, we will be taken away. We serve no use to the Father if we don't produce any fruit. Fruit on a real tree is useful for both humans and the tree. It provides nourishment to eaters as well as a way to spread the seeds of the tree and create more plants. In the same way, our fruit is for others to see and be blessed by as well as to spread the gospel of Jesus Christ. We as believers must be extremely mindful of the fruit we are showing to the world. A tree is known by the fruit it bears and God wants us to be known as His children. What father would not want his child to resemble himself and be accounted for as his own?

Either make the tree good, and his fruit good; or else make the tree corrupt, and his fruit corrupt: for the tree is known by his fruit.
Matthew 12:33 (KJV)

But even if we do bear fruit, the process does not stop there. The book of John highlights that when we do bear fruit, God prunes us so that we will bring forth even more fruit. When you prune a plant, you remove selected parts of it in order to increase the harvest. You remove dead leaves, cut off dead branches and for some plants you cut off what looks like it is good. There is a tree in my parent's front yard that my dad prunes every year. It is quite a large tree but every year my dad cuts off the branches until there is literally almost nothing left. Right after pruning you would think the tree was dead and without hope for producing any kind of harvest. Branches that looked perfectly fine to the naked eye are all chopped off until only the main tree trunk is left. But during the right season, all the branches come back and not only that, they are fuller than before and beautiful white blossoms bloom all over. In your life, you will go through seasons of pruning. God may prune your relationships, your finances, or any other thing you have some attachment to, but it is all in order for you to grow and blossom. Even though it looks rough in the beginning, you can trust that you will have a greater harvest in the end.

I thought this was a great revelation and one we have to constantly remind ourselves of especially when we feel as though God is taking something away from us. Once again, I found my perspective being changed about what I was going through in my life and it would go even further as I felt lead to read the book "Before Saying Yes to the Ring" by Karolyne Roberts (4). After reading I began to write down all the things I learned from it and at that moment I felt the Holy Spirit speak directly to my heart. He told me I needed to de-clutter my heart by removing old memories. I immediately knew exactly what God was talking about.

For several years I had kept memory boxes in which I stored little mementoes from over the years. There were things from significant events in my life like my prom corsage to just things I wanted to look back and remember like love letters and pictures of old friends. I was fond of treasuring special moments and I would just occasionally open up the box and go through the items to reminisce on those times. I knew I would get rid of the stuff eventually because some of the items were from old romantic relationships and I knew it wasn't proper to take those things into marriage. However ,while I was single and free to do my own thing, I had decided to hold on to these things as long as I could. But that moment the Holy Spirit spoke to my heart, I knew He was telling me that I had to go through that memory box and throw that stuff away. I was at work at the time He spoke to me so I wasn't able to complete it immediately but I knew I would definitely pull out my memory boxes and throw everything away as soon as I got home.

It wasn't necessarily an easy task to clear out my memory boxes, but I didn't have too much of a hard time reconciling the thought in my mind. As I was driving home and contemplating the task ahead, God spoke to my heart again. This time He reminded me of all the many pictures I had of old friends and boyfriends that I would also go through from time to time and reminisce. I had tons of pictures on my computer, let alone my Facebook. Did I really have to go through all my pictures and delete them? Now that was hard, and to be honest it didn't make a whole lot of sense to me. I didn't need them but what harm were they to keep? I didn't understand any of the significance but it didn't end there. As I was envisioning all the things I knew that I would be throwing away when I got home, He reminded me of different items that I had that also needed to go. I had gifts of jewelry, clothes, and many other things that held memories of past relationships that I didn't need to have around me to remind me of those times. A lot of the relationships were unfruitful, not to mention hurtful, and even in remembering the good times I couldn't help but remember the bad. In an act of obedience, I was literally about to go home and ransack all that I had to complete this huge purge.

Immediately when I got home I threw away everything in my memory box and deleted pictures of people I was no longer in a relationship with. I went through my closet and other areas and if I found something that held an unfruitful memory then I either put it in a pile to give away or I threw it away. It sounds crazy, and I certainly felt crazy, but I knew for sure I was doing what the Lord wanted me to do. I caught myself being sentimental at times and even trying to justify keeping something I knew I needed to get rid of, but with the help of the Holy Spirit I was able to finish the task. It was hard to let go of some items, some of those items were my favorite things, but nothing was more important than my obedience in that moment. Perhaps the fact that I cared about these material things so much was a tell-tale sign of why I needed to let go of them. That night I prayed and the Holy Spirit spoke to my heart yet again, this time He told me that *memories were weeds*. I wasn't exactly sure what that meant but it was confirmation I had done the right thing so I wrote that phrase down and went to sleep.

The next day I did some research on what a weed is and came up with some interesting facts.

- "A valueless plant, especially one that grows on cultivated ground to the injury of the desired crop." (5)
- They are out of place and not sown intentionally (6)
- They are believed to come from history and were brought in from outside sources (7)

It was after this research that I understood the journey the Lord took me on. In Christians' lives, weeds are anything that affects the ability to bear MUCH fruit. As we read earlier in John 15, it is in the bearing of much fruit that our Father is glorified. Just like in the natural world, weeds inhibit our ability to produce the best fruit and they come from seeds planted in our past. Weeds don't hold any value and they don't belong in our future. They are harmful to us even though they appear powerless. For me, those memories produced fear that choked my ability to have peace about creating new relationships. Those items held memories of past disappointments and hurts in other relationships. While most of those things were not before me daily, reminiscing would only lead me on a mental path that had me thinking about what happened before instead of focusing on the future. I could not allow my mind to travel back to the past to unfruitful memories. I had to bring every thought into subjection.

Casting down imaginations, and every high thing that exalteth itself against the knowledge of God, and bringing into captivity every thought to the obedience of Christ.
2 Corinthians 10:5 (KJV)

God needs a clean, pure heart to dwell in, and because He is the vine and we are the branch, we need Him to abide in us in order to bear MUCH fruit. I know a lot of people may think that it was extreme to throw away all those things, but that was my journey. You may be clinging to something that connects you to something from your past that has no physical component. That's another characteristic of weeds. They will often bloom pretty flowers and you can't tell the difference between the weeds and the plants that are supposed to be there. They disguise themselves and conceal their real purpose. A lot of the weeds in your life may be disguised as something innocent, but what they are really doing is taking the time and the energy that should be used to produce the good fruit found in Jesus Christ.

It takes a lot to truly uproot a weed both spiritually and naturally. I used to hate working in the yard with my mom because a large part of gardening was removing all the weeds. It wasn't as simple as it seemed, you can't just snap off the weed from the stem and call it a day. You have to get deep down in the ground and make sure you pull the weed up from the root or it will come back. And some of those roots are strong and deep and take a lot of effort to pull up from the ground. It is the same with spiritual weeds. As you comb through your life to get rid of the dead weight and weeds, you have to completely remove those things from the root or they will rise up again. Our biblical example of this is found in the book of First Kings with the Prophet Elisha.

So he (Elijah) departed thence, and found Elisha the son of Shaphat, who was plowing with twelve yoke of oxen before him, and he with the twelfth: and Elijah passed by him, and cast his mantle upon him. [20] And he left the oxen, and ran after Elijah, and said, Let me, I pray thee, kiss my father and my mother, and then I will follow thee. And he said unto him, Go back again: for what have I done to thee? [21] And he returned back from him, and took a yoke of oxen, and slew them, and boiled

their flesh with the instruments of the oxen, and gave
unto the people, and they did eat. Then he arose, and
went after Elijah, and ministered unto him.
1 Kings 19:19-21(KJV)

When Elisha was called he didn't just leave everything he had to follow Elijah, he burned both the yoke and oxen that he plowed with. He destroyed every trace to his past. He literally left nothing for himself to go back to. Elisha didn't know Elijah, he didn't even have any details of what was ahead. This plan could have completely back fired but Elisha decided to entirely commit without a plan B. How many of us say yes to God in obedience but leave a way back just in case it doesn't work out? Elisha completely destroyed his former life and just like Elisha, some of us need to completely sever ourselves from our past.

It is imperative that you uproot every inch of those weeds. You can't break off the weed from above ground and move on. Just because it's not visible, doesn't mean that it is really gone. For me it meant getting rid of a lot of physical items that held memories, for you it may mean something else. The important thing is not to leave a way back, whether that is physical or mental. Delete your exes' numbers; you don't need to even provide yourself the opportunity to contact them in your times of weakness. Unfriend that person on Facebook, you don't need to see what's going on in their life. If you want to be free from your weeds, you will have to make major sacrifices in order to remove every trace of it that holds you in bondage.

Once you mature in Christ, the enemy most likely cannot attack you on blatant sin because you will recognize that attack immediately. What we often don't see is when he attacks us by the putting on of weights. He can't stop you altogether but he can slow you down and hinder your fruit through weights and weeds. A lot of us struggle with weeds and don't even know it. I had no idea that my memories held my fear. We are not to dwell in our past, God is not there. God is so good that even if you have no idea what it is that's holding you back, He can search your heart for what needs to be cleansed and renewed.

Search me, O God, and know my heart: try me, and know my thoughts
Psalm 139:23(KJV)

I urge you to let the Lord search your heart today. He wants you to lay aside every weight so He can be glorified. What weight have you allowed the enemy to use to hinder you? It could be memories but it could also be anything else. Jealousy, pride, fear, disbelief, hatred, rage and much more are all forms of weeds that hold part of you in captivity. If you're wondering why you still struggle with such things rising up within you, it's because there's a root somewhere in your spirit that you need to destroy. Those roots are things like unfruitful memories, un-forgiveness, past hurts and rejection. You don't have to keep living with these invisible struggles. I know you're tired of having to deal with these things day in and day out. You can truly be free if you seek God and make the decision to let go.

Don't allow weeds to choke your ability to bear much fruit. Don't allow the enemy any footholds in your life. Close off any door that could lead to a place where he could get to you. Don't leave a way back to the things of old. Purge yourself from anything that could be a hindrance, including unhealthy relationships. Ask the Lord what the weeds are in your life and wait for Him to tell you. Don't think that just because you don't have a memory box, this isn't for you. This lesson is for everyone. It may not be physical items; we have a mental and emotional battle to win as well.

God needs ALL of you. I pray you take this Word, meditate on it and apply it to your life. Part of you cannot be tied up in the past, a person or any material things. Living for Christ requires sacrifice, and it most definitely will require all of you if it hasn't already. God is more interested in where we are going than what happened way back when. We can't move forward and look behind us at the same time. We also can't receive if our hands are closed, holding onto something we don't need. Once you complete the process of letting go, don't pick up those weights again. Make a decision to put them down and leave them there. Be set free so you can experience the fullness of the life God has planned for you both in singlehood and in marriage.

6

Beware of the Decoy

Be sober, be vigilant; because your adversary the devil, as a roaring lion, walketh about, seeking whom he may devour:
1 Peter 5:8 (KJV)

Once you pray a prayer and/or receive a promise from God, there is often a process you must go through in order to experience that promise coming into fruition. During that time, it is highly likely that you will face what I call a decoy test. I got the phrase from my mother who had a word from the Lord one day that simply said 'beware of the decoy'. After looking back on my single season I realized just how relevant that word was. A decoy is anything used to distract, deceive and ultimately prevent you from receiving exactly what God has promised to deliver to you. It is oftentimes a test of whether you will wait for God's best or settle for less. A decoy can be sent out for all different kinds of situations but for those that are single and waiting on your spouse, it is even more crucial for you to know how to recognize a decoy because it is most often a person. Here we will go over some examples of a decoy and how to make sure you are not deceived in your season of waiting.

I personally categorize decoys into two different groups: the *completely wrong* and the *almost right*. Once the enemy knows that you have a promise on the way, you will for sure get a decoy to prevent you from receiving that promise. Some decoys are completely different from what you asked for and some decoys are almost all that you've asked for, but they both are less than God's best for you. Over the years, I've experienced both of these decoys. I've dated guys that were completely wrong for me. Our beliefs didn't match, we didn't have the same values and we didn't have the same goals. For example, I once dated a guy that had no issue with premarital sex. It was against my beliefs and he respected that, but how far could the relationship go with such a difference in conviction? It couldn't go anywhere. Even though he "respected" that I had made a decision not to have sex, he just went and got it elsewhere while we were dating. I had no business going out with him knowing that he didn't share my beliefs in such an important area, but instead of waiting I temporarily settled for what was right in front of me. Something similar is true for Samson in the Bible. Let's take a look at Samson's completely wrong decoy.

And it came to pass afterward, that he loved a woman in the valley of Sorek, whose name was Delilah.[5] And the lords of the Philistines came up unto her, and said unto her, Entice him, and see wherein his great strength lieth, and by what means we may prevail against him, that we may bind him to afflict him; and we will give thee every one of us eleven hundred pieces of silver.
Judges 16:4-5 (KJV)

Now for those that don't know much about Samson, he was an Israelite. Israelites had rules on not marrying outside of their brethren but Samson fell in love with Delilah, who was a Philistine. In his disobedience to his culture and beliefs, Samson pursued a relationship with Delilah. Through this, she was allowed the opportunity to deceive Samson into telling her what gave him his great strength. That great deception is what led to Samson's demise. Delilah was what I call completely wrong for Samson. His relationship with her went against what he knew was the right thing to do, but he loved her. In the same way, it is very easy for us to fall for a decoy that will lead to our destruction as well. I know of many people that have a story of settling for what they knew wasn't right and then suffering because of it.

If you find yourself in a relationship in which you know for a fact that this person is completely wrong for you, get out. You cannot change them and you cannot make it work. Everyone is sent on an assignment in your life and your desperation for love will open you up to being deceived by this wolf in sheep's clothing. The 'completely wrong' decoy can only fool you if you are open to being fooled. It is so far off from what God has for you that you only miss it when you are completely focused on the wrong thing. Do not let your fleshly desires lead you into foolish decisions. There is a reason why the Word of God says we have to kill out the deeds of our flesh. If left untamed, the flesh will control our lives and lead to spiritual death (Romans 8:13). I know it is hard to wait on God's promise but it is not worth the kind of damage this kind of decoy can cause in your life. I thank God for saving me from the people in my life that were sent to pull me away from God. Even when I may have succumbed for a little while, He continued to pull on my heart about what was right. Do not ignore the Lord's pulling and beware of the 'completely wrong' decoy.

The next kind of decoy is one that is much easier to go unnoticed. They are the 'almost right' decoys. They generally have a lot of what you asked for but they are missing some very important components. I had an 'almost right' decoy during the beginning of my purely single season. He was a very nice guy that I had known previously just as friends but he expressed interest in me romantically so I decided to go with it. We were never in an exclusive relationship but we hung out quite a bit and talked every day for about 2 months. For the most part we had fun and most of all He loved God. I hadn't really been exposed to a man that genuinely loved God and was bold about living the Christian lifestyle so I was definitely intrigued. I really thought that there was a possibility that he could be the one God was sending as my husband and I was praying earnestly for confirmation.

As time went on, I found that there were two major things wrong with this scenario. For one, I wasn't attracted to him but I thought perhaps over time somehow it would change. It was always a fear of mine that I wouldn't find a Christian man that I also found attractive.

I got caught up in the hype that attractive men weren't Believers and I thought I would either have to settle or the Lord would miraculously make this man attractive to me. But all the while I would see examples of other Christian women who seemed to find their men extremely handsome and I just couldn't find it in myself to believe that God would choose a spouse for me that I didn't want to be with. Eventually I realized that this particular person wouldn't become attractive to me over time and I didn't have to hold on just because He loved Jesus.

Secondly, my 'almost right' decoy was a distraction. I was still in college at the time and I was also working part-time. I had a lot on my plate and I didn't mind making time to talk to him but it became too excessive. I knew that I wanted a man who would respect my time and set boundaries so that we weren't a distraction to one another and this wasn't it. I constantly had to be the one to end conversations and pull away so I could complete my responsibilities as a college student and employee. I didn't have time to stay up all night on the phone or text all day during class. I could tell this was an issue for him. I knew for sure that this was another confirmation that this relationship wasn't God's best for me. Anything that God has ordained will not distract you from taking care of your responsibilities. Anyone who wants excessive amounts of your time at the expense of your time needed to sleep, work, and do other mandatory tasks is not what God has in mind for you. I could have settled for a man that was passionate about Jesus, that I wasn't attracted to and didn't value my time in the way I wished but I thank God once again for steering me away from that. These were two things that were very important to me. In the midst of seeing some of what I wanted in a man, I could've overlooked what was missing and missed God's best for what was just good enough.

The biblical example of the 'almost right' decoy goes back to the example of the tribes of Israel that we already discussed in Chapter 3. In Numbers Chapter 32, the tribes of Reuben and Gad looked at the land they were in and decided to ask Moses if they could just stay there instead of crossing over the Jordan River with the other tribes. The Bible says these two tribes had a multitude of cattle. I can only guess that it must have been very important to them to have room for their cattle in their new homeland. Unsurprisingly, before they reached the promise they were intercepted by an 'almost right' decoy in the form of land with enough space for their cattle. They knew there was a promised land for all the tribes of Israel over the Jordan River but they decided to stop where they were. The tribes could certainly survive on this land and it was important to have space for their cattle, but it was less than what God had promised them. They allowed themselves to be distracted and gave in to their own feelings of disbelief.

For the 'almost right' decoy you have to be extremely in tune with God to make sure that you are not deceived. No one is perfect but there are some things you should know that you cannot compromise on, no matter how much of the other qualities are embodied. It's really easy to let a few good things out shadow the bad, even if the bad is truly not what you want. The Lord has your best interest at heart and would never give you a spouse or a blessing that didn't measure up to His expectations. While you could possibly have a good life with the 'almost right' decoy, you can't experience the *best* life with this decoy. You can easily make the wrong decision to compromise on something that's very important to you and end up disappointed.

In the same way, there are so many other examples of settling for something that's almost right. If you know you asked God for something specific but something less than that is presented to you, you should seek God to make sure you aren't being fooled by the 'almost right' decoy. Exactly what you wanted could be coming down the pipeline but you decide to take less than what you asked for and less than what God was willing to give. There is a plan for you that is God's best, but you have to be in alignment with His Will to actually experience what that is. Know what qualities you cannot compromise on based on Godly standards and remember to beware of the 'almost right' decoy.

Now that we can identify what a decoy is and some of the different forms they can come in, let's talk about how to make sure we don't fall victim to this trap. One of the best pieces of advice I probably ever received in regards to deception is to have vision. Let's see what the Word of God has to say about the subject of having vision for your life.

And the LORD answered me, and said, Write the vision, and make it plain upon tables, that he may run that readeth it.[3] For the vision is yet for an appointed time, but at the end it shall speak, and not lie: though it tarry, wait for it; because it will surely come, it will not tarry.
Habakkuk 2:2-3 (KJV)

Where there is no vision, the people perish: but he that keepeth the law, happy is he.
Proverbs 29:18 (KJV)

The Bible says that not only are we to write the vision, but vision is so important that without it people can be led astray. When you have vision for your life, it gives you a bulls-eye of sorts. You know what you want and more importantly, you know what you don't want. I'm not a proponent of making some extensive list of what you want in a spouse but I strongly encourage all single people to have a vision written out for their husband/wife. I wrote a vision for my husband around the age of 20 and I also have a vision for my life in general, things like what I want to accomplish in ministry and career-wise. You need some tunnel-vision in order to block out all the distractions and easily discern any decoys that are sent your way. It can save so much time and trouble if you are able to quickly determine whether someone or something fits into your life's vision or not and take the necessary course of action without any confusion. If that person, business deal, or ministry opportunity doesn't line up with the vision God has given you, then you don't have to waste your time even considering it. You will get different things thrown at you on the course of life so it's really easy to become distracted from reaching your goals and believing for God's promises. As with all things, I cannot encourage you to write a vision outside of what God wants. Everything listed should be Godly standards and you should seek the Lord on what vision He has for your life before you go and make up your own.

Another safeguard against the deception of a decoy is to make sure you are maintaining your relationship with the Lord. It is through that relationship that you are able to heighten your discernment and have the level of faith needed to wait patiently on the Lord to fulfill his promises. Paul tells us in the book of 1

Corinthians the connection between our relationship with God and our ability to discern.

But the natural man receiveth not the things of the Spirit of God: for they are foolishness unto him: neither can he know them, because they are spiritually discerned.
1 Corinthians 2:14 (KJV)

Once you become saved, you are given the gift of the Holy Spirit. The bible calls the Holy Spirit the Spirit of Truth because He is our connection to being able to hear from God (John 16:13). When we have a relationship with God, He will speak through the Holy Spirit to show us how to differentiate between the rights and the wrongs in our life. It is when we are living after the flesh that we cannot receive from the Spirit of God and we end up being deceived. In order to secure your ability to hear from the Spirit of God, you must maintain your relationship with God through prayer, studying the Word of God and worshipping. When you are in a solid relationship with God, you can be sure that you have the necessary tools to see beyond the natural circumstances and make the right decisions.

The decoy test is all about your patience and faith. If you are patient enough to wait on God to fulfill His promise, you will not fall for the deception of any of these decoys. You can feel confident in placing all of your faith in God and His Word. He will not fail and He cannot lie (Numbers 23:19). It is when you are impatient and focused on your own inabilities that you open yourself to being deceived. You may be reading this and have already settled for less than God's best in some area of your life. But fortunately for us, God works everything together for our good. The Word of God says that you still have the hope of God making it right for you (Romans 8:28). For those that have read this and want to renew their commitment to waiting on God's best, be sure to remember to write out your life's vision, maintain your relationship with God and remain alert at all times so that you are not tricked by the decoys of life.

7

God's Perspective

Grace and peace be multiplied unto you through the knowledge of God, and of Jesus our Lord,[3] According as his divine power hath given unto us all things that pertain unto life and godliness, through the knowledge of him that hath called us to glory and virtue:

2 Peter 1:2-3(KJV)

While you journey on the road of life, your mindset will ultimately shape your reality. The way that you think controls both your words and actions and therefore dictates the course of your life. We can look at the Word of God to clearly tell us the relationship between what we think, what we say, and the things we experience.

For as he thinketh in his heart, so is he: Eat and drink, saith he to thee; but his heart is not with thee.
Proverbs 23:7 (KJV)

A good man out of the good treasure of his heart bringeth forth that which is good; and an evil man out of the evil treasure of his heart bringeth forth that which is evil: for of the abundance of the heart his mouth speaketh.
Luke 6:45 (KJV)

Death and life are in the power of the tongue: and they that love it shall eat the fruit thereof.
Proverbs 18:21 (KJV)

There is a progression here that I want you to follow and be sure to remember.

1. What we believe in our heart dictates the kind of person we are

2. What is in our heart, is manifested in our words
3. Our words have power, both to create and to destroy

It is clear when looking at the three aforementioned verses that it is imperative that we learn to correct our thoughts so that we can experience a greater level of God's blessings in our lives. Believe it or not, a lot of people are incorrect in their thinking about the way God operates and consequently have trouble trusting God to keep His promises. That distrust leads to many of the things we've gone over already in the previous chapters like fear, loneliness, discontentment and disobedience. The key to truly aligning our thoughts with God's will and being able to receive the promises of God that we haven't received yet is to understand God's perspective.

Before we delve further into seeing those promises from God that we're waiting on, we have to clarify what it really means to trust God. I love the definition of trust found on dictionary.com, it reads that it is "reliance on the integrity, strength, ability, surety of a person or thing". So, the first thing we need to do is align our minds with the thought that we aren't trusting in the action of God doing something for us, we are trusting in who God is. We have confidence in God knowing that He is faithful (1 Corinthians 1:9), He doesn't lie (Numbers 23:19), He has all the power (Psalm 62:11) and much more. Instead of focusing on whether or not He will bring us our spouse or whatever else it is that we want him to do, we have to put our trust in who He is.

When I was in college, I had a full academic scholarship that took care of all my expenses. Everything went great until my junior year when I noticed that my scholarship wasn't activated in my account. I tried to wait and see if there was a glitch but school began and my scholarship never posted to pay the balance of my tuition and housing. I sat in the federal aid office for hours on end and finally was told that the school didn't have the money and that they were working to resolve the issue. I was shocked and I didn't know what to do. I needed books, and other supplies and I didn't have the money to cover it because I was depending on the supply I got from the scholarship. I remember calling my parents, trying to figure out what we could do and we all decided that we were just going to trust God to work it out. Because we knew God was faithful, we knew He wouldn't bring me to school on scholarship and leave me halfway through to fend for myself. Because we knew God had all the power, He had the ability to work this situation out and help them obtain the money they needed to cover my scholarship.

While it sounds like it was so easy to trust God, it wasn't. The problem wasn't fixed overnight. I got emails and letters about eviction from housing and paying the tuition bill constantly and I ran into other people in the same situation who were pretty discouraged. In spite of all that, I trusted in who I knew God to be. Finally after a few weeks, the scholarship cleared and I was able to take care of everything I needed. I wasn't focused on God paying my bill; I was focused on what I knew about God's character. I didn't know anything besides who my God was and it allowed me to experience peace in the midst of waiting for God to fulfill His promise.

So the question then arises, what do we do when we feel like we're trusting God to keep His promises and we still don't see it happening? I did a study in 2012 of how God operates and I think it's important to try to gain a better understanding of it. He works from a completely different perspective than what we see here on Earth so first let's take a look at the book of 2 Peter to see the key to understanding God's perspective.

Grace and peace be multiplied unto you through the knowledge of God, and of Jesus our Lord,[3] According as his divine power hath given unto us all things that pertain unto life and godliness, through the knowledge of him that hath called us to glory and virtue:[4] Whereby are given unto us exceeding great and precious promises: that by these ye might be partakers of the

divine nature, having escaped the corruption that is in the world through lust.
2 Peter 1:2-4 (KJV)

In verse 3 it says through God's divine power He has already given us all things we need for life and for godliness. 'Hath given' is used in past tense, so we have to note here that the Bible is telling us that everything we need for our life, both naturally and spiritually, has already been given to us. It also goes on to say in verse 4 that exceeding great and precious promises have already been given to us as well, once again given is in past tense. A lot of Christians do not view God as having already done everything for us; I know this may be hard for people to wrap their minds around. God is not going through each day with us surprised at what happens and scrambling to fix our problems. God sits outside of time, meaning He doesn't operate based off of our clock and calendar. He presides in eternity where He can see beyond this current moment. As humans, we don't automatically think of God in this way because we can only see what's right in front of us. If you need to, take a moment to meditate on this verse and reshape your thinking to take your previously known boundaries off of God and see Him in the light of this new perspective.

As I continued my study on God's perspective, 3 verses stood out to me that further confirmed that it is true that God operates outside of time. Read each verse and see if you can also notice the common phrase they all carry.

Blessed be the God and Father of our Lord Jesus Christ, who hath blessed us with all spiritual blessings in heavenly places in Christ:[4] According as he hath chosen us in him before the foundation of the world, that we should be holy and without blame before him in love:
Ephesians 1:3-4 (KJV)

And all that dwell upon the earth shall worship him, whose names are not written in the book of life of the Lamb slain from the foundation of the world.
Revelation 13:8 (KJV)

Forasmuch as ye know that ye were not redeemed with corruptible things, as silver and gold, from your vain conversation received by tradition from your fathers;[19] But with the precious blood of Christ, as of a lamb without blemish and without spot:[20] Who verily was foreordained before the foundation of the world, but was manifest in these last times for you,
1 Peter 1:18-20 (KJV)

If you didn't recognize it, the common phrase here is "foundation of the world." In each verse it says that God did something before the foundation of the world. From this, we understand that before Adam and Eve were even created, God had carried out the actions on His part. He chose us to be in Him from the beginning and the Word of God also tells us that Jesus was slain from the foundation of the world. Before Adam and Eve brought sin into the world, God's plan for salvation had already been carried out. I know you're wondering how this is possible since there was such a difference in time between when Adam and Eve sinned and when Jesus came into the world as flesh, but 1 Peter 1:20 is the game changer.

1 Peter 1:20 says that though Christ was foreordained before the foundation of the world, He was manifested in this world at a certain time for us. Jesus Christ had already been chosen to be slain but we didn't see that happen in the flesh until an appointed time on Earth and that time was chosen for the benefit of us. We have established that God is all-knowing (Psalm 147:5) and He sits outside of time in eternity where He is not bound by time like we are (2 Peter 3:8). Where we are in the natural world, is different from the spiritual realm where God is. This is clearly illustrated in the book of 2 Corinthians.

While we look not at the things which are seen, but at
the things which are not seen: for the things which are
seen are temporal; but the things which are not seen
are eternal
2 Corinthians 4:18 (KJV)

In his infinite wisdom, God sees both the beginning and the end. He saw exactly what we would need and according to what we've already read in 2 Peter 1, He provided those things. The thing is, those promises were completed in the eternal realm where we can't see them with our natural eye. What we await in the natural realm, where we currently live and operate, is what we call the manifestation of the thing that God has already done in the spirit. I know this is a lot so just take your time and feel free to meditate on what you have already read. The major point of God's perspective is that He has already completed everything we could ever need for this life. We just have to experience that manifestation in the Earth.

Since we know God is not in time with us, He is not unable to see tomorrow like we are and He is certainly not unwilling to give us His promises, why would we not experience Him filling those promises? Why would we not have the spouse we've prayed for or the situation worked out for us already? Considering that God has already provided everything we need in the spirit, there are only two reasons we would not be experiencing the fulfillment of our prayers and His promises: it isn't time yet or we aren't in alignment to receive those things. While the promises are already done for us, as with Jesus in 1 Peter 1:20, they manifest at certain times for our benefit. As hard as it may be to accept, you may not have something just because it isn't time for you to have it yet.

There is an appointed time for everything to happen in your life and it all works according to what God knows is best. No matter what you do, you cannot change that time.

On the other hand, you may be out of God's will and He is unable to give that promise to you because you aren't in position. Bad decisions, sin, and distractions can all take you away from where you need to be and then prevent you from receiving God's promises. God may have your spouse for you, but since you've decided to date someone outside of His Will, He can't bring them to you. Or God may already have the solution to your problem on its way to you, but you got impatient and tried to fix it yourself so He can't deliver it to you in the same way. Thankfully, no matter how far off you've gotten from God's plan, He can always bring you back again through the guidance of the Holy Spirit. All is not lost. He will welcome you back with open arms. Don't be discouraged, God can reroute you back to where you need to be so you can experience the answer to your prayers.

His promises never change; it's us that cause them to be hindered in their delivery from the spirit to the natural.

So how do we access these divine promises that we know are waiting to be manifested for us? Through confessing the Word of God back to God in faith. We find whatever it is we need in God's Word and then in prayer we confess in faith that we have those things. If we need healing for our body, instead of praying and telling God we are sick, we find a promise for healing like Isaiah 53:5 and we say it out loud in prayer. Faith comes by hearing …Through this act of faith, we are expressing belief that we are already healed and that God just needs us to believe it so He can give it to us.

We must pray and operate in our lives from God's perspective. We are not moving God's hand when we pray but only getting ourselves in the right position to receive what we're asking for and using our words to show God the faith we have in Him. At the very beginning of this chapter we discussed the power of words and what's in our heart. When the Word of God is in your heart, it will come out of your mouth and bring forth the good you want to experience in your life. All we need is faith in God and His Word combined with the power of our tongue to see a change in our circumstances. One of my favorite scriptures about prayer gives a very encouraging sentiment to what we've been discussing, it's found in the book of 1 John.

And this is the confidence that we have in him, that, if
we ask any thing according to his will, he heareth
us:[15] And if we know that he hear us, whatsoever we
ask, we know that we have the petitions that we desired
of him.
1 John 5:14-15(KJV)

When we pray according to God's will, He will hear us and grant the petitions we desired of Him. We know we are praying according to God's will when our prayers line up with the Word of God. Whatever you need from God has already been completed on His behalf, what He is waiting for is for our faith to match what He's trying to give us so we can see that promise come to fruition. That is why Jesus would ask people if they believed He could do something before He did it. There is an example of that found in Matthew when Jesus healed two blind men.

And when Jesus departed thence, two blind men
followed him, crying, and saying, Thou son of David,
have mercy on us.[28] And when he was come into the
house, the blind men came to him: and Jesus saith unto
them, Believe ye that I am able to do this? They said
unto him, Yea, Lord.[29] Then touched he their eyes,
saying, According to your faith be it unto you.
Matthew 9:27-29(KJV)

God wants you to know that according to your faith, it will be done unto you. You don't have to worry about the details of how God will fulfill His promise to you because He has actually already done it. He isn't withholding anything from you for no good reason, but only waiting on you to trust Him. Will you believe that God has already taken care of what you are waiting on and just have faith that He will bring it to pass at the right time? When your faith and the timing of God coincide, you will see God deliver your blessing. So remember to trust in who you know God to be and not what He is going to do for you. And if you don't know enough about God to be able to trust Him in that way, take some time to get to know Him through prayer and studying of the Word of God. Also, remember that your words have power and they will be governed by what's in your heart. Guard your heart with all diligence, because out of it will flow either the good or bad that you experience (Proverbs 4:23).

Change your perspective from thinking that you are waiting on God to do something and rejoice in the fact that you have a God that loves you so much that He already has plans in place to take care of you. Be encouraged that you serve a good and awesome God who is beyond willing to bless you with the desires of your heart. I'll leave you with one last verse to remember as you pursue the faith and patience you need to experience the blessings of the Lord.

Wait on the LORD: be of good courage, and he shall strengthen thine heart: wait, I say, on the LORD.
Psalm 27:14(KJV)

8

The Secret to Waiting

*But the LORD said unto Samuel, Look not on his
countenance, or on the height of his stature; because I
have refused him: for the LORD seeth not as man seeth;
for man looketh on the outward appearance, but
the LORD looketh on the heart.*
1 Samuel 16:7(KJV)

I've talked a lot about perspective and focus in your life up until this point because what you put extensive amounts of focus on will consume you. If you focus on work too much, you'll be a workaholic; if you focus on the negative too much, you become depressed and so on and so forth. The same is true for you when you focus on something like being single, especially in the wrong light. It's a very simple equation but too often we end up with a negative result instead of a positive one. As you find yourself waiting for any of God's promises, whether it's a spouse or not, you may go through seasons where you feel like the promise doesn't look any closer. You can perceive decoys, you're staying away from discontentment and your focus is on God, but you can't help but wonder why you are still in this phase of waiting. I know from experience that it can be quite draining to feel like you're waiting on God to do something when you've done all you can, so I wanted to touch on one important thing that the Lord does for all of us in our journey to the promise: test our heart.

A main reason that there is lag time between being given a promise and actually experiencing that promise is that God wants to show us what's in our heart. You can only see the outside, but as we see in 1 Samuel 16:7 God looks at the heart. Many people may think that God tests us to show Himself whether we are ready for the promise or not, but God already knows everything so that can't be true. If you take the time to pay attention to yourself along the journey to promise, you will realize how the Lord is revealing your own self to you so that you can grow. It is under times of pressure that what's inside of us begins to come out and be visible. If you never squeeze an orange, you wouldn't know that the orange contains juice. Your hands provide a pressure that forces what's inside the orange to come outside of it. In the same way, a potter must apply pressure to clay in order to shape it into the piece of work he is trying to create. Just like that, the journey to your promise is a tool for God's use in making what He already sees in your heart visible and then shaping you into the person He needs you to be in order to receive your promise.

Without ever testing us, we would never get to the core of our humanness and be able to see things we need to either change or make better use of. Many people were tested in the Bible during their promise journey. Just as an example, I want to highlight the trying of both Joseph and King Hezekiah so let's get started with Joseph.

He sent a man before them, even Joseph, who was sold for a servant:[18] Whose feet they hurt with fetters: he was laid in iron:[19] Until the time that his word came: the word of the LORD tried him.
Psalm 105:17-19 (KJV)

For those that don't know the story of Joseph, here's a brief synopsis. He was given a dream that he would rule over his brothers and in their jealousy, they sold Joseph into slavery. From that time on, Joseph experienced many ups and downs including going from captain of the guard to a prison inmate off of false accusations. Through all of this, the Lord was with Joseph and he ultimately became second in charge to Pharaoh and ruler of Egypt. You can find the detailed story of Joseph in the Word of God in Genesis Chapters 37-50. Joseph waited many years between when he was given a dream that he would rule over his brothers and coming into command under Pharaoh. The great Joseph we read of and talk about so much had a promise journey too. That journey wasn't filled with easy times nor was it shortened because Joseph made the right decisions.

As you read the story of Joseph, there were several moments where he honored God in the midst of extremely hard times, but it still took time to see that vision come to pass. We find the purpose of that time in Psalm 105. The Word of God says that until it was time for Joseph's promise to come to pass, the Lord tested him. We have no entries in the Word that Joseph 'deserved' anything that happened to him and we also have no notes of him making the wrong decisions in his tests. I can only surmise that the ups and downs of Joseph's journey were meant to pull out the greatness that was inside of him. He was ridiculed by his brothers even though he was chosen as the favorite son by his father. In order to be a great ruler, he needed to know what God had placed on the inside of him. We see through this journey Joseph's commitment to being faithful to God, his trustworthiness, and the revealing of his gift to interpret dreams. Without the journey, Joseph may not have realized those qualities or been given the opportunity to develop his gifts before the lives of thousands of people depended on it. You may have been single for years and living righteously but God still has a journey for you to go through. You could be waiting on God to fulfill a vision He gave you ages ago even though you've been trying your best to walk in your God-given purpose. Don't look at other people and think it's unfair, or it's only taking so long because you've done something to deserve it. Sometimes, you have to just let go of what it seems like on the outside and trust God that He is only using this time to prepare you for a great promise.

As for our example of King Hezekiah, the exposure was slightly different but all for the same purpose. Our main verse is 2 Chronicles 32:31 but I have included 2 Kings 20:12-13 as a little bit of a backstory as to what's going on.

At that time Berodachbaladan, the son of Baladan, king of Babylon, sent letters and a present unto Hezekiah:

for he had heard that Hezekiah had been sick.[13] And
Hezekiah hearkened unto them, and shewed them all
the house of his precious things, the silver, and the
gold, and the spices, and the precious ointment, and all
the house of his armour, and all that was found in his
treasures: there was nothing in his house, nor in all his
dominion, that Hezekiah shewed them not.
2 Kings 20:12-13 (KJV)

Howbeit in the business of the ambassadors of the
princes of Babylon, who sent unto him to enquire of the
wonder that was done in the land, God left him, to try
him, that he might know all that was in his heart.
2 Chronicles 32:31(KJV)

We find King Hezekiah as a very successful king with lots to show for it. If you read up a few verses you will see that Hezekiah struggled a lot with pride and had already been tested in this area (2 Chronicles 32:24-26) after he was healed from a disease that was purposed to take his life. We see him again after that test, in all of his prosperity, and he was visited by people who knew he had been sick and wanted to see the wonders the Lord was working in the land. Unfortunately, pride was once again lifted up and instead of showing forth his God, Hezekiah found it more important to show them every ounce of his treasure. On the outside, it looked like the princes were

101

just visiting to bring Hezekiah gifts and well wishes, but 2 Chronicles 32:31 says that the Lord used this as a test of his heart. The prophet Isaiah later tells Hezekiah that because he had chosen to show those men all of his things, all of it would be taken away from him. How would we know that Hezekiah had truly humbled himself if he was never tested in this area? God uses situations in our life to show us what we still need to work on and for Hezekiah it was pride.

Sometimes in the midst of your promise journey, the Lord will test you to show you the destructive things that are in your heart. Without tests, you would be going along on your journey thinking everything is ok, when in fact you have corrupt ways and thinking patterns that you don't even know are there. Just from examples in previous chapters alone, I have learned during my waiting times that I can be selfish, self-righteous, impatient, lacking in faith and so much more. They weren't easy pills to swallow, but if I want to walk in the Lord's goodness, those things had to be brought to my attention so they can be submitted to the Lord in prayer and fixed. The Lord is concerned about the condition of your heart, but all you see is Him not fulfilling a promise or bringing you your spouse. This journey is about maturing and it doesn't always feel good when you're under the shaping and molding of the living God. When it gets hard or like Hezekiah you are tested and realize God is showing you something you need to change, focus on learning the lesson that God is trying to teach you.

Your only visible perception of the orange we talked about earlier is the peel on the outside, but if you leave it at that you miss the nourishing fruit on the inside and the juice that can be used for a multitude of purposes. Your only vision for the potter's clay is the formless mass it is currently. Without the shaping on the potter's wheel, you miss the awesome things this one piece of clay can turn into. Thank God we serve a God that sees beyond what we can see and only sees us in a positive light (Jeremiah 29:11). He saw an Earth without form and void and spoke its promise of greatness instead of condemning it for its lifeless state. He saw darkness but spoke light. He saw the Earth void but spoke to create living creatures to inhabit it (Genesis 1). How many of us could use the Lord's help in being more positive about our promise journeys? Can we decide this day to choose to look at the season of waiting as a positive time of development instead of a time of torment and affliction? Can we try our best to actually learn from the tests and the waiting instead of just trying to get through it and get it over with?

God is going to continue working on you to make you more into His image whether you like it or not. He looks past both our exteriors and our current state and sees us as His completed work which He has promised not to stop perfecting until the day of Jesus Christ (Philippians 1:6).

The secret to waiting is realizing that it's a learning experience that holds great importance in your personal and spiritual development. It doesn't last forever, but it holds a significant purpose within your process to fulfilling God's will for your life. You can't see what lies ahead but God can and He wants you to be ready. There is always a bigger picture, but we often get stuck looking at what's right in front of us. God's tests are always about purpose greater than us. Hezekiah's failure led to a Babylonian siege that affected the whole kingdom of Israel. Joseph's triumph led to years of provision for the whole tribe of Israel. Pass the test for you and for those around you that will be affected by it. Always seek to take God's perspective and remember He has no plans to harm you. Waiting can be really hard, but patience in this life is so necessary. Remember that God is just using this time to shape you and mold you into the man or woman of God that He has called you to be. Pay attention to what He is trying to show you and teach you. One day soon enough you will have the promise you've been waiting for and realize it was so worth it for God to take the time to prepare you for it.

9

Purity…Heart, Mind and Body

I beseech you therefore, brethren, by the mercies of
God, that ye present your bodies a living sacrifice, holy,
acceptable unto God, which is your reasonable service.
Romans 12:1 (KJV)

Of course I couldn't write a book encouraging singles as well as all those who are waiting on God's promises without touching on the subject of purity. I know that in the mind of most people, they think of purity and it automatically means not having sex outside of marriage. But I wanted to talk about the subject from a different angle. While purity does include not engaging in sexual activity before you are married, that is only one of the results of being pure and not the sum total of what it means. Contrary to popular belief every person is called to purity, not just single people.

Beloved, now are we the sons of God, and it doth not yet appear what we shall be: but we know that, when he shall appear, we shall be like him; for we shall see him as he is.[3] And every man that hath this hope in him purifieth himself, even as he is pure.
1 John 3:2-3 (KJV)

Whether you are single and waiting for your spouse, married, or just anticipating God's promises in your life, you have a commission to be pure as the children of God. We have a hope of seeing our Savior and being transformed into His image in its entirety and because of that hope we choose every day to live a lifestyle of purity. To be pure means to be uncontaminated, untainted, and free from foreign or inappropriate elements (8). Imagine a clear glass full of water, or you can perform this experiment if you so choose. If you place an object on the other side of it and look through the glass, chances are you can see the object. It may be distorted because of the reflection but you can see it decently well. If you shine a flashlight through it, you should be able to see the light come through on the other side. Now if you were to begin to add dirt to the water in the glass, the water starts to become cloudy. You can't see the image on the other side and the light shining through the glass will get dimmer. In reality the glass is you, the water in the glass is your soul, the light shining through you is Christ and the image on the other side of that glass is God. When you add the dirt of the world, you become contaminated. The light of Christ cannot shine in your life and your ability to see God fails. And this is not only for you, but for those looking to you who should be able to see the Christ in you and be led to God. All that we've discussed so far is useless if you do not choose holiness and righteousness to live a pure life before God.

So we hear all the time that we live in this world but we aren't of it (John 17:15-16) but how do we maintain this standard of purity? First, we have to start off by knowing that we are made pure through Jesus.

When he said above, "You have neither desired nor

taken pleasure in sacrifices and offerings and burnt
offerings and sin offerings" (these are offered
according to the law), ⁹ then he added, "Behold, I have
come to do your will." He does away with the first in
order to establish the second. ¹⁰ And by that will we
have been sanctified through the offering of the body of
Jesus Christ once for all.
Hebrews 10:8-10 (ESV)

Under Old Testament law, they had to commit sacrifices every year to be sanctified and made holy. But through Jesus, a sacrifice was made once and for all, that we could be holy and in right standing with God forever. As a follower of Jesus Christ, I am a believer that it is only through Jesus that we are made holy and it is only through Him that we can live a pure life. You cannot do it on your own. The first step in the direction of purity is making sure that we have experienced true salvation or everything else we try to do will fail. There is a salvation prayer in the introduction of this book that you can go through if you're not sure that you've ever really given your heart to the Lord.

After we accept Jesus as our Lord and Savior, to live pure as followers of Jesus Christ means in its totality what we see presented by Paul in Romans 12:1.

I beseech you therefore, brethren, by the mercies of

God, that ye present your bodies a living sacrifice, holy,
acceptable unto God, which is your reasonable service.
Romans 12:1 (KJV)

We cannot go through life expecting to experience God's best, avoid deception, hear God's voice and have the mind of Christ without fully surrendering to God. Paul's statement begins with the word 'beseech' which is an urgent plea for us to take heed to his instructions. To live as a follower of Christ is a life of constant sacrifice. Sometimes you can't go to the places you used to go to or hang out with the people you used to hang out with because they aren't living for Jesus like you are. We sacrifice ourselves on the altar of who God has called us to be. So obviously to be pure is <u>not an action</u> but the result of our choice to sacrifice our lives to God and live a holy and acceptable life before Him.

I hear people say all the time that they want to stop cursing, stop lying, stop cheating, stop having sex outside of marriage, etc. but the problem is that they are focused only on actions. You'll have such a hard time trying to change an action rather than changing what's causing that action to come forth. Part of being a sacrifice is death. We don't sacrifice our lives to God literally and die, rightly divide me. But if you are still producing sin, what is still alive to produce that sin? Is that memory of someone hurting you allowing anger to rise up and let you lash out at people when they do you wrong? Is that root of rejection causing you to be coldhearted towards people when they come into your life? What part of yourself have you held back in the sacrifice? Only things that are living can produce, so we have to make sure we've given God EVERY part of us. If we feed our flesh, we can expect it to give birth to evil actions, thoughts and words. When we present our lives to God as a living sacrifice, it is every single part of us. We mortify the deeds of the flesh and should therefore produce things of the spirit, not the flesh (Romans 8:5). If you're trying to change something, make sure you are pulling that weed up from the root and not just trying to snap it off from the surface.

It sounds so straightforward to choose to be pure but in the world we live in it is especially difficult. A lot of times it goes unnoticed because we're so conditioned to the dirt that we are desensitized. Honestly, we live in a society where obscene behavior is glorified and rewarded. We see, hear and experience so much of the world that we lose our ability to discern between righteousness and sin. We would much rather justify what we're doing using the world as our measuring stick than be told we're wrong according to the standards in the Word of God. Purity is just as important now as it ever was and if you're reading this book right now then God wants you to commit to living purely.

Every time we turn on the TV, get on social media, or even leave the house we run the risk of the dirt of the world being poured into our glass bit by bit. The Bible talks about the need to protect our hearts, bodies and minds.

Keep and guard your heart with all vigilance and above all that you guard, for out of it flow the springs of life.
Proverbs 4:23 (AMP)

What? Know ye not that your body is the temple of the Holy Ghost which is in you, which ye have of God, and ye are not your own? [20] For ye are bought with a price: therefore glorify God in your body, and in your spirit, which are God's.
1 Corinthians 6:19-20 (KJV)

So brace up your minds; be sober (circumspect, morally alert); set your hope wholly and unchangeably on the grace (divine favor) that is coming to you when Jesus Christ (the Messiah) is revealed.
1 Peter 1:13 (AMP)

As we navigate through life, we will no doubt come into contact with the world and run the risk of being contaminated with their lifestyles. In order to stop this from happening, you have to constantly watch over your soul by protecting yourself from things that could contaminate it. Be aware of what you're seeing and what you're listening to and make a conscious effort to control those things. I know for a while I was watching a hit show on television that I loved. I would watch it religiously and often couldn't wait until each episode every week but soon the scenes became too graphic and vulgar. As a single Christian woman, I couldn't expose myself to constant sex scenes, adultery, and a slew of other explicit things on a weekly basis. It wasn't good for me and it certainly wasn't lending itself to maintaining a pure mind and spirit. You would think that it would be easy to let go of, but it wasn't. I saw everyone's posts about how good the show was and what happened that episode and I wanted to watch so badly but I knew I couldn't. I made the decision to stop in the name of my desire to live pure before God. I'm not bashing anyone for choosing to watch what they want to watch on television, but make sure all that you do is supportive of you living a pure and holy lifestyle.

No matter how much we talk about being Christians and following Jesus, we will be affected by the world we live in. For most of us, we have to work, we have to interact with people and we have to live life outside of our homes, so some of it will be outside of your control. But thanks be to God who has provided a way to

wash the dirt of the world off every day and that is
through the Word of God.

Husbands, love your wives, even as Christ also loved
the church, and gave himself for it;[26] That he might
sanctify and cleanse it with the washing of water by the
word, [27] That he might present it to himself a glorious
church, not having spot, or wrinkle, or any such thing;
but that it should be holy and without blemish.
Ephesians 5:25-27(KJV)

Sanctify them [purify, consecrate, separate them for
Yourself, make them holy] by the Truth; Your Word is
Truth.
John 17:17(AMP)

It saddens me to hear of all the people who don't
take advantage of God's Word. They only open it on
Sundays, if that, and quote it occasionally on social media
accounts so everyone else can think they read it. Not only
is it our manual for living, but it's essential to our being
able to live a holy lifestyle. Just like water, as we read and
study the Word of God, the dirt of the world is washed
away and we become the clear, clean vessels we need to
be for God's use. You can't experience God's promises
without purity and you can't live true purity without the
Word of God.

I had to be sure to include this chapter in a book on singleness and waiting for God's promises because as a whole it often goes unaddressed. We want God to give us all of these things but we aren't willing to give Him ourselves first. Purity of heart, mind and body is essential to the Christian life. It's not just about sex or what you watch on television either; the weeds we addressed earlier like un-forgiveness, jealousy, and hatred can all cause us to be contaminated and unable to see and hear God. You have to make a conscious decision to live holy and set apart for God's purpose.

You must take on the responsibility of protecting your eyes and ears. Remember to stay in the Word of God so you can be cleansed each and every day. If you want God's best in your life, you have to give Him your best. If you're holding on to any area of your life, it's time for you to let it go. That includes your desires for marriage, children and whatever else if you desire them more than you desire God. You sacrifice what you want because what God wants is more important. It is our reasonable service, the least we can do for a God who has given so much for us, to give ourselves completely to Him and submit to His plan for our life.

10

A Little Encouragement

*The LORD is good unto them that wait for him, to the
soul that seeketh him.*
Lamentations 3:25 (KJV)

The vast majority of Christians in the world are in a phase of waiting on God to do something. You are certainly not alone if that is you. We are constantly in a state of need and dependency on God and I think that is purposed by God to help us to continuously grow. In spite of this, we can't be so focused on waiting for God to do that one thing for us that we miss out on what else the Lord is doing. We can't be constantly looking for tomorrow and then never fully present in our today. So I wanted to end this book on an encouraging note about the good God is doing while we anticipate our time of fulfillment.

Too many people are waiting on something to happen before they start living life. Life does not begin when you get a certain job, a certain salary, a spouse, or whatever else you are asking God for. Life is going on right now, right in front of you, and God is moving outside of the petitions you have up before Him right now. We serve a God that can multi-task. I've heard people say they're waiting on kids to buy the house they want or waiting on a spouse to travel to the places they've always wanted to go to. Of course be led by God in your finances and whatever else but why miss out on the joy of the present? Go out and do all the things that you wanted to do! You aren't required to live half of a life because just one of God's promises hasn't come to fruition yet.

I have been so blessed during this single season that I can't even begin to explain it all. I wrote a 5 year vision when I was 20 of all the things I wanted to do by the time I was 25 years old. At the time I am writing this, my 24th birthday is just about 2 months away and I would say at least 75% of those things I asked God for are done. I graduated from college, bought my first house, found my purpose and now I'm finishing my first book. All of which were written down in 2011. I want to be married and have a family and all that good stuff but my life isn't lacking because I'm single and yours doesn't have to be either as you wait on God's promises. God is still doing awesome things for me and in my life.

I love Lamentations 3:25 that says that the Lord is good to those that wait on Him. That's a promise! The wait time between now and seeing the answer to that prayer is still a time where you can receive goodness from the Lord. You don't have to stare at the clock and be stagnant as you wait for your time to come. Your time is now! You know what the Bible says about being caught up in your tomorrow?

So do not worry or be anxious about tomorrow, for tomorrow will have worries and anxieties of its own. Sufficient for each day is its own trouble.
Matthew 6:34 (AMP)

Let tomorrow take care of itself. At some point you have to stop planning and start doing. You have been given the gift of today. What are you going to do with it? God is moving in your life at this very moment. Are you going to take the time to look up and see it? Or focus on what He hasn't done yet? You'll most likely ALWAYS be waiting on something from God, it doesn't mean you stand still and wait. You keep moving and you'll run into God's promises as you go. If you don't, one day you'll look up and realize that life passed you by while you were waiting for it to start. Whatever you are believing God for will happen at the right time, all you have to do is trust God and keep pushing.

I truly hope you have learned something as you read through some of my personal stories and the lessons about waiting that I have learned along the way. I want you to learn from my experiences so that you don't have to take the time and energy to go through it yourself. I don't want you to miss out on anything God has for you and I certainly don't want you to view this season of waiting as an awful period in your life. Don't forget that there is purpose behind everything, so view your life through the lens of God's perspective. God loves you and wants you to experience the best life possible. Your job is to trust Him and walk in His will for your life, not worry about what He is or isn't doing for you. No matter what you are waiting for, don't let it stop your life from moving forward. There are people connected to your life just waiting for you to find your purpose and go after it. Let go of everything holding you back and realize all the greatness that lies both ahead and within you. Lay all your cares at the feet of Jesus and step into the SON-shine. He is waiting for you and so am I.

References

1. McMillan, John Mark. "How He Loves". *The Medicine.* John Mark McMillan & Integrity Media, Inc., 2010. CD.

2. "Content." *Merriam-Webster.com.* Merriam-Webster, n.d. Web. 14 Jan. 2015. <http://www.merriam-webster.com/dictionary/content>.

3. "Discontentment." *Dictionary.com Unabridged.* Random House, Inc. 14 Jan. 2015. <Dictionary.com http://dictionary.reference.com/browse/discontentment>.

4. Roberts, Karolyne. *Before Saying Yes to the Ring.* IAMImage LLC, 2013. Print.

5. "Weed." *Dictionary.com Unabridged.* Random House, Inc. 14 Jan. 2015. <Dictionary.com http://dictionary.reference.com/browse/weed>.

6. Lingenfelter, Dwight, and Nathan Hartwig. "Introduction to Weeds and Herbicides."*Penn State College of Agricultural Sciences Cooperative Extension.* The Pennsylvania State University, 1 Jan. 2013. Web. 15 Jan. 2015. <http://pubs.cas.psu.edu/freepubs/pdfs/uc175.pdf>.

7. Lauritsen, John. "Good Question: Where Do Weeds Come From?" *CBS Minnesota WCCO-TV.* CBS Local Media, a Division of CBS Radio Inc., 30 July 2012. Web. 15 Jan. 2015. <http://minnesota.cbslocal.com/2012/07/30/good-question-where-do-weeds-come-from/>.

8. "Pure." *Dictionary.com Unabridged.* Random House, Inc. 14 Jan. 2015. <Dictionary.com http://dictionary.reference.com/browse/pure>.

Made in the USA
San Bernardino, CA
21 February 2015